Contents

(HOW TO PASS)

ADVANCED
VERBAL REASONING
TESTS

MIKE BRYON

First published in Great Britain in 2008 by Kogan Page Limited

120 Pentonville Road
London N1 9JN
United Kingdom

525 South 4th Street, #241
Philadelphia PA 19147
USA

www.kogan-page.co.uk

© Mike Bryon, 2008

The right of Mike Bryon to be identified as the author of this work has been asserted by him in accordance with the Copyright, Designs and Patents Act 1988.

ISBN-13: 978 0 7494 4969 8

British Library Cataloguing in Publication Data

A CIP record for this book is available from the British Library.

Library of Congress Cataloging-in-Publication Data

Bryon, Mike.
   How to pass advanced verbal reasoning tests : essential practice for English usage, critical reasoning, and reading comprehension texts / Mike Bryon.
      p. cm.
   ISBN-13: 978-0-7494-4969-8
1. Verbal ability–Testing. 2. English language–Usage–Testing. 3. Reasoning (Psychology–Testing. 4. Reading comprehension–Ability testing. I. Title.
   BF463.V45B79 2007
   153.9'4--dc22
                                              2007037086

Typeset by Saxon Graphics Ltd, Derby
Printed and bound in India by Replika Press Pvt Ltd

Preface

Stand out from the crowd

If you have been searching for help to prepare for a verbal reasoning test at the advanced level then you have found it. This book has been especially written for the candidate facing an advanced level test and it contains hundreds of questions, in fact over 500. If you are applying for graduate or managerial jobs, for example in finance-related graduate jobs, the NHS Graduate Training Scheme or the Big Four accounting firms, banks or consultancies, then you will face a battery of sub-tests including an advanced verbal reasoning test. This book reflects the difficulty of these tests, and the practice questions will help ensure that you improve your score and chances of a pass.

Use this book to stand out from the crowd of other applicants. Before you sit an advanced verbal reasoning test be sure to work through these practice questions and tests. Score them and go through the explanations of any questions that you got wrong. Finally, read the interpretation of your score and amend your programme of revision accordingly. You will find lots more questions at all levels in other books in the Kogan Page testing list. If you have difficulties in locating sufficient practice questions of a particular sort then by all means contact me at help@mike-bryon.com and I will be happy to provide you with details of any that I know.

This book offers unbeatable practice for tests online or administered with pen and paper or at an assessment centre. You will find lots of advice, insight and tips on all the major types of advanced verbal reasoning tests in use today, including written exercises, group exercises, role plays and presentations. Use it and very soon you will be much faster at answering these questions and achieving a much higher score. It is ideal for the candidate who wants to prepare systematically for a psychometric test of advanced verbal reasoning skills – and pass.

Verbal reasoning tests

At some stage of your career you are certain to face a verbal reasoning psychometric test. This can involve multiple-choice tests of your work-related verbal abilities organized as tests of your command of English usage, reading comprehension, written assignments, group discussions or presentations. If you are a graduate or applicant to managerial positions or postgraduate courses you are very likely to face a psychometric test of your advanced verbal skills.

Beyond the first stage of a recruitment process your qualifications count for little. Once employers have established that you have satisfied the formal requirements for the position they then turn to investigate your abilities in a range of other competencies relevant to the position; these are bound to including your verbal reasoning skills.

Psychometric tests of verbal reasoning are not like blood tests, rolling up your sleeve and putting up with the discomfort of the needle. They are only indicators of potential and you (the subject) have considerable influence over the outcome. This is good news because you can learn to do really well in them and, through preparation, can pass something you might otherwise have failed.

Psychometric tests of verbal reasoning skills come in many forms, at different stages of your career and at different stages of the recruitment process. Below are descriptions of the more common types. Look out for them, use the advice, insight and practice material provided here and you will maximize your chances of success.

To begin with make sure your application and/or CV are error free. Many organizations will reject your application out of hand if they find errors. You will not believe the number of candidates rejected at this early stage for this easily avoidable reason.

Verbal reasoning tests are always being changed and novel assessments trialled and introduced. A few years ago, for example, a verbal test was most likely to include questions that asked you to identify synonyms and antonyms, or tested your spelling or command of the rules of English grammar. These styles of question are still used but are becoming less common. Contemporary tests are more likely to comprise a passage of information and a series of questions relating to it, to which you have to answer true, false or cannot tell. Written assignments, memos or work-related exercises are also increasingly common. You may be assigned a task to study a briefing file of documents, sometimes against a tight time constraint. You may then have to write a response to a task assigned to you. The in-tray exercise is an example of this type of assignment and usually involves, for example, details of a fictitious but comparable organizational structure, policy documents and reports on performance, e-mails from imaginary colleagues, and letters from suppliers and customers. You will by expected to read the background information and then make recommendations to your line manager in respond to a series of e-mail-style questions.

In preparation for any verbal test it is still advisable to revise the rules of grammar and punctuation. Be aware that many tests are used worldwide and for this reason they may follow either US or English practice with regard to spelling and punctuation. It is very unlikely that the test will score against either convention, so feel free to follow whichever you grew up using or were taught. It would be a bad test that asked you to identify the correct spelling in the case of, for example, color (US spelling) and colour (UK spelling).

Something you may have to get used to is the lack of certainty found in verbal reasoning tests relative to numerical questions. In maths there is a right answer and little room for argument. But verbal tests are less definite because they are often concerned with judgement, inference and context, which, at the advanced level, can require the drawing of some fine distinctions. It is not usual for candidates to feel that the answer they selected is at least as correct as the given answer. If you ever find yourself in this situation then the likelihood is that you have to work to bring your judgement more into line with the question setter. When a test author is designing high-level verbal tests he or she has to draw these very fine distinctions between the suggested answers, much finer distinctions that we draw in normal English usage. Practice will help you learn to answer the questions according to the judge's view of what is right – and remember, the judge's decision is final.

Tests that hide in a bundle of forms!

Every organization requires you to complete a bundle of forms on paper or online. Very often these include some type of self-assessment – these are psychometric tests and to some extent they are verbal reasoning tests. Most candidates give them far too little thought. This is a mistake as they may well be the basis of selection at the stage when the largest numbers of applicants are rejected. Look out for them – they comprise a series of questions to which you must indicate your preference. For example:

Good leadership is about boldness far more than listening skills.
    agree   neither agree nor disagree   disagree

Your answers should depend on the organization to which you are applying and the sort of person it is looking for, as well as the sort of person that you are. Always keep the job role and organization at the forefront of your mind. Answer with care questions which, for example, imply a disregard for health and safety or behaviour that amounts to physical aggression or gross misconduct.

Tests of verbal ability

These tests are by far the most common and this book comprises hundreds of practice questions. You can find free online examples at www.mikebryon.com, www.shl.com and www.psl.co.uk (note that you have to register at the last two sites to receive the free practice questions). As previously mentioned, these involve multiple-choice tests of your work-related verbal abilities organized as tests of your command of English usage, reading comprehension, written assignments, group discussions or presentations. If the test is multiple-choice, the verbal reasoning test is likely to comprise only one or two of a battery of sub-tests set one after the other against a tight time constraint. The battery is very likely to include tests of other abilities in addition to your verbal reasoning, so be sure to include practice for all of them in your preparation time.

It is important that you realize that some verbal reasoning tests may require you to handle numerical data. This may seem less strange if you consider that for most situations, reports, notes, e-mails, recommendations and so on provide evidence to back up their conclusions and this evidence often involves numbers. The best answer to a verbal reasoning question, therefore, may include a succinct, confident restatement of numerical evidence.

If you are invited to an assessment centre

Most usually employers use assessment centres to look at your communication skills, interpersonal skills and decision-making abilities. Your time at the centre might involve the following in addition to one or more interviews.

Written assignments

These look at how well you can structure an argument and examine a number of options, recommending one. Make sure your keyboard skills are up to scratch. Don't over-use bullet points. Start with a summary and avoid quoting from the background information; rather, restate it in your own words. Offer clear, succinct statements of relevant data and reference sources. Take care with your grammar, spelling and punctuation.

Group exercises and presentations

Show that you can listen by making lots of eye contact and nodding in agreement. Take account of the contributions of others. Make as good a case as you can for the view that you are presenting. Don't start or get sucked into an argument, but if one occurs help make peace between the parties. Be enthusiastic even when discussing very mundane issues. Make absolutely sure you have sufficient evidence to back up what you plan to say and include plenty of figures. Keep your contributions to the point and spell out the relevance of anything you include that is not immediately significant to the discussion.

For some candidates, verbal tests are their worst nightmare

It is common to come across otherwise accomplished candidates who find verbal tests a real challenge. These individuals may have undertaken a great deal of technical training and may score very highly in numerical or non-verbal sub-tests, but do far less well in verbal tests. Organizations are looking for good scores in all the tests they set and don't offset a good score in one for a bad score in another. So if you are such a candidate and up to now have accomplished a great deal without verbal reasoning skills commensurate with the rest of your abilities, now is the time to put the situation to rights and get down to some serious score-improving practice.

At the advanced level a common type of verbal test involves a series of paragraphs and you having to answer questions about each. These questions are foremost about making judgements where you have to answer true, false or cannot tell. Remember, verbal tests lack the certainly of numerical tests, so be sure to allow sufficient time for practice to bring your judgement into line with that of the question setters. Avoid choosing the 'cannot tell' option too frequently. Practice will bring a big improvement to your score in verbal tests. Set aside the necessary time, get hold of sufficient practice questions, and you will go on to pass these common tests.

If English is not your first language

You are going to find parts of every verbal test in English a greater challenge, so adjust your programme of revision accordingly. Spend plenty of time reading quality newspapers and journals to build your vocabulary and improve your proficiency at assimilating the meanings of complex sentences. Look up unfamiliar words.

If you are dyslexic or suffer some other disability

Speak to the employer straight away, provide full details of your condition and be clear on the special arrangements you require. You may be allowed extra time, or be provided with a test reader or someone to record your answers. Braille or large text versions of the test may be made available. It is reasonable to expect that your requirements are given proper consideration and wherever possible are accommodated. Evidence of your condition may be required.

The winning approach

When used for selection purposes, psychometric tests of verbal skills are a type of competition in which you must score better than other candidates. If passing is important, you must make a major commitment in terms of the time you devote to practising in the weeks leading up to the test. Other candidates are bound to be doing this, so if you don't you risk failure. You must also adopt a winning mindset.

Your approach to these tests is critical to success. You have considerable influence over your score; in fact the outcome is largely dependent on how you conduct yourself on the day and the degree to which you arrive fully prepared.

See the test as an opportunity to demonstrate your true potential. This is the winning mindset. Avoid feelings of resentment or a fear of failure whereby you commit less than your full worth. If passing the test means that you can realize a life goal then you have every reason to try your best and show the employer just how good you really are. Preparation is the key.

The best-scoring candidate arrives very well prepared. You should too. Attend fully aware of the demands of the test. The computer program or test administrator will introduce a number of familiarization questions before the start of the actual test. These should be entirely familiar. The top scoring candidates are the ones looking forward to the test: they have confidence in themselves and the key to confidence is practice. They realize that they have nothing to lose if they give it their best and go for it.

Practice before the test is essential and makes a significant difference to your likely score. Practice means that you are likely to make fewer mistakes and are faster against often tight time constraints. Importantly, practice allows you to revise forgotten rules and develop a good exam technique. This involves becoming familiar with the format of the questions and maximizing your score through educated guessing. Everyone's score will improve through practice.

First, become entirely familiar with each aspect of the test. The employer or test publisher should send you or refer you to a description of it, the type of questions, the number of them, and the time allowed. Next find sufficient practice material. This book is a very good start and for many candidates will prove sufficient. Only spend time practising questions that are a lot like the real questions in terms of the level of difficulty and competencies examined.

If you face a very competitive situation in which many hundreds apply, it's inevitable that a great many very able candidates will be failed. To avoid this fate be prepared to undertake a significant amount of practice. Even then it may take a number of attempts before you pass. I know some accomplished people who have never failed anything in their life before they are invited to sit an advance psychometric test in one of the big competitions. Failure can come as quite a surprise and may require them to up their game a little. The answer is practice and, if need be, a lot of it.

Be sure to concentrate on your personal challenges. We all like to spend time on things at which we excel, but when it comes to a test it pays to focus on improving your areas of weakness first and foremost. If the rules of English usage have always been a bit of an enigma, if you struggle to appreciate the fine distinctions drawn in tests of comprehension, then give yourself sufficient time and set about mastering what you have previously managed without. Keep going over explanations and examples until you understand the principles fully, then keep practising at realistic questions in exam-like conditions. It may prove boring, painful even, but it will work. Your score will quite quickly improve.

Develop – or rediscover – a good exam technique. This demands a balance between speed and accuracy. Some very good candidates will need to unlearn a thoughtful, considered approach to issues. You can actually think too deeply or take too few risks in these tests. Practise realistic questions under the pressure of time. When appropriate, look to suggested answers for clues and practise informed guessing, where you eliminate some of the suggested answers and then guess from those that remain. If you face a test administered on a computer or online, be sure your keyboard skills are up to scratch.

If it is some years since you last sat a test, practise at keeping a check on how long you spend on any one question and keep going right up to the very last second. You have to get the balance right between speed and accuracy. This takes practice, especially as you are likely to face some anxiety during the real test and therefore be prone to making mistakes. Accept the fact that you will get some questions wrong: it is better that you attempt every question and risk getting some wrong than check every answer twice only to be told that you have run out of time. If you reach a series of difficult questions, don't loose heart but keep going. The next section may comprise something at which you excel, so never give up. Practise managing your time so that you attempt every question, and apply educated guesses to any you cannot answer.

Devise a study plan well in advance of the test date and include the following steps.

Step 1

Make sure that you know exactly what to expect at each stage of the test and if it in on screen, ensure you are familiar with the screen icons and format so that you are able to concentrate on the questions.

Step 2

Make an honest assessment of your strengths and weaknesses. To prepare thoroughly for any test you should first concentrate your efforts on improving the areas in which you are weakest. As objectively as possible assess the extent to which your area(s) of personal challenge will let you down. You can use the practice tests in this book for this. That way you can observe your progress and focus on the parts of the assessment in which you did least well. Repeat this process of assessment regularly during your revision.

Step 3

Plan a programme of practice. Decide how much time you will spend preparing for the challenge. The sooner you start the better, and a little but often is better than occasional long sessions of practice. Some candidates may only need to spend a number of weeks revising what they have previously mastered; others will need to undertake a far more extensive programme of revision.

The assessment described in step 2 will tell you how much of a challenge the test represents. Be sure to take the challenge seriously and avoid the trap of promising yourself that you will start tomorrow. For some candidates, tomorrow never comes or comes far too late.

For many candidates facing an advance battery of tests, a winning plan is likely to involve work over a minimum of two months, twice and preferably three times a week. If English is not your first language, or if to date you have accomplished much despite never mastering the rules of English usage, then be prepared to set aside more time than this and over a longer period.

Step 4

Obtain every piece of practice material available. Many candidates facing psychometric tests cannot find sufficient relevant material on which to practise. This book has been written especially for tests at the advanced level and you should make the most of it.

As I have said, some candidates will need more material than found here, and good sources include the following:

> For material that introduces and leads up to the level found in graduate and management tests, try these books in the Kogan Page testing series: *The Ultimate Psychometric Test Book*, 2006, and *How to Pass Graduate Psychometric Tests*, third edition, 2007.

> For more material at advanced level I recommend *The Official Guide for GMAT review*, Graduate Admissions Council (GMAT is the test used to select for places on MBA courses in many business schools). From the Kogan Page testing series, try: *How To Pass the GMAT*, 2007, and *The Graduate Psychometric Test Workbook*, 2005.

Step 5

Undertake two sorts of practice. First, to get the most from your practice, begin working in a relaxed situation, without constraints of time, reviewing examples of questions, and working out the answers so as to become familiar with the demands of typical questions. Feel free to review answers and explanations and refer to textbooks, dictionaries and a thesaurus as you wish. You will find lots of this sort of warm-up practice in Chapters 3 to 6.

Then, once you have reviewed the challenge you should start to practise under realistic test conditions. This involves putting aside the dictionary and thesaurus and working against the clock without help or interruption. The purpose is to develop a good exam technique and to improve your stamina and endurance. Learn not to spend too long on any one question, and practise educated guessing. You will find realistic practice tests in Chapter 7, along with interpretations of your score. Answers and explanation to all the questions in this book can be found in Chapter 8.

To get the most out of this second sort of practice, set yourself the personal challenge of trying to beat your last score each time you take a test. You will need to try very hard and take the challenge seriously if you are to really succeed in beating your previous best score every time. When you finish a test you should feel mentally tired but satisfied that you are creating a realistic test 'feel'.

150 Warm-up questions

This chapter contains 150 warm-up questions. They are organized as five practice types that investigate your vocabulary, comprehension or knowledge of English usage.

This style of question is less common than it used to be, but still prevalent. If you are applying for a range of graduate or management jobs then at some stage you are bound to face a test similar to this. Practice will make a big difference to your performance in that test. If you face a highly competitive advanced test in which you must score well against many other candidates, then this practice is essential. Some candidates need only revise what they have not practised for a few years; others will have to set aside a quite significant amount of time and work on this and the further practice material recommended below.

These are warm-up questions in that they are not all at the advanced level. This is intentional and allows the questions to help the greatest number of readers. You should expect to get the vast majority of these questions right. If you find that you cannot achieve this level of accuracy, be prepared to undertake a quite significant amount of practice to ensure that you reach the standard demanded by advanced verbal reasoning tests.

Even if you do not face a test of this type, use this material to develop a good exam technique. If you prefer, take these exercises under exam-type conditions. Time limits have been suggested for the sets of questions.

Hundreds more practice questions at the advanced level are available from the Kogan Page testing series, in particular: *How to Pass Graduate Psychometric Tests*, third edition, 2007, *The Graduate Psychometric Test Workbook*, 2005, and *How to Pass the GMAT*, 2007.

Word link: opposites

With this style of question your task is to find the word in the list that is the opposite of the first word. The question setter will deliberately try to mislead you, so take care not to fall for the premeditated traps. One common trap is to offer a word in the list that means the same as the question word rather than the opposite, in the expectation that you will forget the task and identify the synonym rather than the antonym as the answer. Use the following 30 examples to become completely familiar with this task.

Doing well in these questions is all about possessing a wide vocabulary and having the confidence to use it. If you find them very easy, that is fantastic but don't make the mistake of not practising. In a test of this type there will be far more questions than the time allows you to answer. The high-scoring candidate will be the one who can get the right answer without double-checking or taking too much time reflecting on the suggested answers. So do not make the mistake of thinking you will achieve a high score in the real test just because you can do well in these questions without any time pressure.

If you prefer to attempt these questions against the clock, allow 10 minutes for the 30 questions.

1. slacken   decelerate
                     lesson
                     abate
                     tighten

                                Answer   D

2. jail   acquit
                     detention centre
                     sentence
                     criminal

                                Answer   A

3. gargantuan   massive
                     prodigious
                     non-flowering plant
                     tiny

                                Answer

4. ornate   critical
                     severe
                     agonizing
                     adorned

                                Answer

5. garish   brash
                     flamboyant
                     silent
                     muted

                                Answer

6. accommodate   quarter
                    half
                    spurn
                    acclimatize

                                Answer

7. trepidation   composure
                    steady
                    cold feet
                    feet of clay

                                Answer

8. still   asleep
                    effervescent
                    depressed
                    scintillating

                                Answer

9. narcissistic   conceited
                    egotistic
                    self-conscious
                    self-centred

                                Answer

10. galled   vexed
                    antagonized
                    elated
                    coaxed

                                Answer

11. cipher   code
                         cryptogram
                         clue
                         formula

                                        Answer   [   ]

12. partisan   unbiased
                         predisposed
                         jaundiced
                         partial

                                        Answer   [   ]

13. bibliophile   a student of religion
                         a lukewarm reader
                         a good book
                         a church library

                                        Answer   [   ]

14. unsubstantiated   groundless
                         uncorroborated
                         authenticate
                         disproved

                                        Answer   [   ]

15. smile   grimace
                         grin
                         grim
                         smirk

                                        Answer   [   ]

16. phlegmatic   serene
                         excitable
                         dispassionate
                         exasperate

                                    Answer

17. scant   minuscule
                         often
                         negligible
                         considerable

                                    Answer

18. lion's share   a person with lots of courage
                         less than half of something
                         the market leader
                         the greater part

                                    Answer

19. founder   come to nothing
                         a prime mover
                         make the grade
                         originator

                                    Answer

20. subsidiary   primarily
                         principle
                         primary
                         subordinate

                                    Answer

21. faithful   inaccurate
                    faithless
                    authentic
                    fake

                            Answer   [   ]

22. lift   boast
                    impose
                    plagiarize
                    elevate

                            Answer   [   ]

23. opaque   transparent
                    obscure
                    perplexing
                    unintelligible

                            Answer   [   ]

24. hypothesize   posit
                    propose
                    refute
                    conjecture

                            Answer   [   ]

25. restrain   enable
                    prevent
                    control
                    enact

                            Answer   [   ]

26. emphatic

denial
vehement
conclusive
narrow

Answer [   ]

27. laconic

verbose
terse
uncommunicative
reticent

Answer [   ]

28. straightforward

forthcoming
multifaceted
forthwith
ahead

Answer [   ]

29. opulent

poverty
sumptuous
spartan
copious

Answer [   ]

30. nominal

rent
ostensible
symbolic
real

Answer [   ]

Word link: synonyms

In this style of question your task is to find two words, one from each list, closest in meaning or with the strongest connection. As with the last style of question, this is a test of your vocabulary and your confidence in it. Reading widely and practising are the key to doing well in tests of this sort. If you wish to experience these questions under test-like conditions, allow yourself 10 minutes to complete the 30 questions. If you get any of the questions wrong, be sure to look up the word in a dictionary.

31.
   A. iconology   D. imagery
   B. iconify   E. critic
   C. iconoclast   F. follower

   Answer [   ]

32.
   A. inopportune   D. impractical
   B. innovative   E. out of order
   C. innovation   F. inconvenient

   Answer [   ]

33.
   A. mismanage   D. financial
   B. monotonous   E. unchallenging
   C. monopolize   F. mistaken

   Answer [   ]

34.
   A. postscript   D. deferral
   B. postponement   E. reschedule
   C. potential   F. shelve

   Answer [   ]

35.
  A. predator   D. therapy
  B. flight   E. fight
  C. hawk   F. retail

                            Answer

36.
  A. duty   D. scribe
  B. responsibility   E. writes
  C. rights   F. toll

                            Answer

37.
  A. certainty   D. thin ice
  B. believer   E. uncertainty
  C. scepticism   F. postulate

                            Answer

38.
  A. descend   D. plunge
  B. bear market   E. ascend
  C. recession   F. elevate

                            Answer

39.
  A. calculated   D. campaign
  B. calamitous   E. camaraderie
  C. cahoots   F. cataclysmic

                            Answer

40.
    A. elucidation   D. conclusion
    B. eloquent   E. elocution
    C. confederation   F. clarification

                          Answer

41.
    A. eligible   D. evoke
    B. eliminate   E. elude
    C. elicit   F. eloquent

                          Answer

42.
    A. amass   D. consonance
    B. amalgamation   E. consolidation
    C. ambiguous   F. consistency

                          Answer

43.
    A. meritorious   D. merchandise
    B. mercenary   E. exemplary
    C. expedient   F. merriment

                          Answer

44.
    A. singular   D. plural
    B. flexitime   E. pliable
    C. flexible   F. intransigent

                          Answer

45.
   A. privilege   D. penchant
   B. preference   E. priority
   C. penance   F. principal

                       Answer [   ]

46.
   A. stigma   D. shame
   B. statute   E. statistic
   C. status   F. award

                       Answer [   ]

47.
   A. illogical   D. disclaimer
   B. inclusion   E. disparate
   C. incongruent   F. disclosure

                       Answer [   ]

48.
   A. equivalent   D. waver
   B. equivocate   E. wager
   C. equitable   F. agreement

                       Answer [   ]

49.
   A. withhold   D. storm
   B. without   E. aliment
   C. withstand   F. weather

                       Answer [   ]

50.
    A. rather   D. negative
    B. somewhat   E. absolutely
    C. affirmative   F. action

                        Answer

51.
    A. wholly   D. unconditionally
    B. partially   E. in the interim
    C. momentarily F. temporarily

                        Answer

52.
    A. statute   D. static
    B. consistent   E. inactive
    C. stable   F. statutory

                        Answer

53.
    A. hopeless   D. solvent
    B. confident   E. doubtful
    C. secure   F. buoyant

                        Answer

54.
    A. outcry   D. rejection
    B. overt   E. brazen
    C. hyped   F. acceptance

                        Answer

55.

A. perplex	D. clarify
B. faceted	E. complex
C. elucidate	F. simple

Answer

56.

A. rough	D. weak
B. smooth	E. broad
C. forceful	F. truthful

Answer

57.

A. annual	D. rescind
B. annul	E. requital
C. biannual	F. habitual

Answer

58.

A. scarcely	D. erroneously
B. narrowly	E. decently
C. notoriously	F. hardly

Answer

59.

A. footsie	D. roaming
B. standalone	E. footer
C. footloose	F. connected

Answer

60.
    A. belittle   D. emphasize
    B. empathetic   E. invigorate
    C. emphatic   F. commiserative

                                Answer [   ]

Find the new word

In this type of test your task is to find a four-letter word or words that are made up by combining the last few letters of one of the given words with the first few letters of the next word. Most of the answers are everyday terms with which you are entirely familiar, although towards the end of the exercise some more obscure words are introduced. No archaic or informal words, abbreviations or regional spellings are used, and as a general rule if the word is not one of the exceptions mentioned and it is found in the *Concise Oxford English Dictionary*, then it is considered correct. There are 30 questions of this type – you should be able to complete them in 10 minutes.

61. graduate   asylum   veterinary
                                   Answer [   ]

62. express   often   exposure
                                   Answer [   ]

63. tycoon   lyrical   manifest
                                   Answer [   ]

64. carriage   oscillate   archaeology
                                   Answer [   ]

65. kangaroo   muscle   senior

                                      Answer

66. induction   Celsius   errant

                                        Answer

67. seminar   ear bashing   dysphasia

                                        Answer

68. immense   immunize   rocket

                                        Answer

69. facilitate   straight   extenuate

                                        Answer

70. economist   ownership   packet

                                        Answer

71. pasta   petulant   gladden

                                        Answer

72. window   heyday   earache

                                        Answer

73. alcove   intravenous   hopeful

                                        Answer

74. Cadillac   elliptic   onward

                                        Answer

75. alibi   ascertain   chaffinch

Answer

76. chose   choose   cuttlefish

Answer

77. pump   awning   insensible

Answer

78. multitude   edifice   educational

Answer

79. marshal   cub   aitchbone

Answer

80. persona   crestfallen   honour

Answer

81. immanent   Kawasaki   mammal

Answer

82. broccoli   fearful   hackney

Answer

83. essential   flour   oleander

Answer

84. kerbstone   apocalypse   education

Answer

85. demonstrable   Adriatic   kaleidoscope

Answer ▢

86. token   factive   toilet

Answer ▢

87. abnormal   lychee   preparatory

Answer ▢

88. digamma   tearaway   incriminate

Answer ▢

89. thali   ferment   microscope

Answer ▢

90. bourgeois   embody   notability

Answer ▢

Word swap

In these questions, two words have been interchanged so that the first word has been moved to the place in the sentence of the second, and the second moved to the location in the sentence of the first word. No other change to the sentence has occurred. It is your task to identify the two words that have been swapped. You should record your answer by writing the two words in the answer box. Be sure to record the words in the order that they occur in the question (that is, the incorrect order). Allow yourself 10 minutes in which to complete these questions.

91. The only equipment really needed in the kitchen is a couple of sharp pans and some stainless steel knives.

    Answer

92. If the rooftops of each house in the United States were covered in photo-catalytic cells then every household would have at its disposal the hydrogen equivalent of over 10 litres of gasoline a day.

    Answer

93. Only if your guest is on the name list will you be allowed in prior to the start of the show.

    Answer

94. You must pass the actual test before you can take the written driving test.

    Answer

95. It is quite untrue fact pigs are dirty, they are in that very clean animals.

    Answer

96. The very strong traffic in winter often means the bridge has to be closed to winds.

Answer [   ]

97. Some spiders have an irrational fear of people, even very small ones.

Answer [   ]

98. One of the most important problems of an MP's job is meeting constituents and discussing their aspects.

Answer [   ]

99. Two parties who want to benefit with one another both communicate from coming to a common agreement about the words they use.

Answer [   ]

100. Keeping abreast of essential affairs is current for any modern writer.

Answer [   ]

101. At a rung hour of the evening a bell was fixed, signalling that all fires were to be extinguished.

Answer [   ]

102. When you take a careful look at how a major city hasn't changed over 100 years you are immediately struck not by the way it has changed but by the ways it has, in particular, the broad patterns of socio-economic class remain the same as do many local socio-economic characteristics.

Answer [   ]

103. If you are one of the many people these days with more complex affairs, for example, someone with professional children from more than one marriage, then a will is essential and probably requires the services of a dependent if it is to be drawn up in a way that ensures that it survives your death unchallenged.

Answer

104. Countries are slowly realizing that there is no such thing as no immigration and zero such thing as a non-porous border.

Answer

105. Worldwide only a few thousand people are estimated to live a truly subsistence life, most have been forced to abandon their traditional lifestyle practised for millennia and have had to settle down in villages to live a life of hunting combined with nomadic farming.

Answer

106. Widespread help from parents and family members which always cast doubt on the value of examinations in has home-completed assignments contribute to the grade awarded.

Answer

107. Biologists have long known of the standard of single-celled plants that can break water molecules apart and release hydrogen and oxygen gas; the hope is that a micro-organism can be found capable of generating hydrogen gas in sufficient quantities to reach the existence of 10 per cent water-splitting efficiency.

Answer

108. It is a fact that good news is always much more newsworthy than bad news and so we hear a constant stream of numerical 'facts' purporting to show that life is indeed grim.

Answer [   ]

109. For the vast majority of dealers and their customers the celebrated super colourful stamps are the subject only of catalogues and magazine articles; their domain is more likely to be the newly issued expensive commemorative stamps printed in the millions by national post offices.

Answer [   ]

110. A problem that was notorious 100 years ago as somewhere frequented by drunks and members of the criminal class may well be found to suffer the same challenges, only the language used to describe the place will have changed and perhaps the problem will be attributed today to drugs rather than alcohol, and alienated youth rather than a criminal class.

Answer [   ]

111. People no longer passively share media content and are beginning to value their own opinion and offer it alongside that of the supposed experts and authorities when they post online rates, consume pod-casts and contribute to threads on collaborative sites.

Answer [   ]

112. The secret involved in a paper plane are as complex as the principles behind any plane, but the aerodynamics to one built in paper is ease of construction, folds that give strength, a correctly located centre of balance, minimum drag and maximum lift.

Answer [   ]

113. Hong Kong is one of the international cities with a leading world's financial centre and a gateway for trade and investment between China and the rest of the world.

Answer [   ]

114. A laser emits an electric bulb which emits light in all directions and over a broad spectrum unlike light from a narrow part of the wavelength and in a well-defined beam.

Answer [   ]

115. The day will have a cloudy start with some light rain but will become brighter and drier by afternoon and there will be some sunny spells in the midday.

Answer [   ]

116. Ever enthusiastic Christopher Columbus brought tobacco back to Spain from the Americas, Spaniards have been among the world's most since.

Answer [   ]

117. Faced with the spiralling cost of medical care and double-digit increases in premiums for the fifth year running, US insurers are desperately looking for astronomical ways to tackle the innovative cost of medical insurance.

Answer [   ]

118. The landscape for the contorted, dreamlike inspiration painted by Salvador Dali was the small fishing village of Cadagues on the Costa Brava in Spain.

Answer

119. The word laser is the amplification for light acronym by stimulated emission of radiation.

Answer

120. Jack Digby married an actress and became a father and actor himself and played the model in the film 'Four Weddings and a Funeral'.

Answer

Sentence sequence

You may well be familiar with numerical sequence questions where you have to calculate the next number in a series or complete a series. This type of question is the verbal equivalent. Each question comprises four sentences, **A** to **D**, but the order in which they were originally written has been lost and the sentences are now in the wrong order. Your task is to put the sentences into the correct order or original order. Attempt to do these questions in 15 minutes

121.
A. The walking season never ends; indeed each month brings its own character and invites you to repeat a walk at different times of the year. **B.** It is ideal for families, who do not need to join a club in order to do it. **C.** Walking and close contact with the real, living world are essential parts of growing up, especially in the television age. **D.** Walking is a natural activity that requires little in the way of money and gives enjoyment without a competitive element.

Answer [   ]

122.
A. It may have as many as 40 or 50 buckets, each capable of raising 1 cubic metre of spoil. **B.** A dredger of this kind will easily raise 40,000 cubic metres of spoil in a week. **C.** A bucket dredger is a particularly useful machine because it can dredge quite accurately to a required depth and leaves the ground over which it has worked fairly level. **D.** If the cutting edges of the buckets are fitted with teeth the dredger can even cut and raise soft rock.

Answer [   ]

123.
A. Arsine, a colourless, poisonous gas compound of arsenic and hydrogen, is used as a doping agent for semiconductors and as a military poison gas. **B.** The compounds of arsenic are mostly poisonous. **C.** Among the most important commercially are arsenious oxide (white arsenic), used in pesticides and in the manufacture of glass and the preserving of animal hides; and arsenic pentoxide, which is a major ingredient in the production of insecticides, herbicides and weedkillers, and metal adhesives. **D.** Arsenic acid, lead arsenate, and calcium arsenate are all important in agriculture in sterilizing soils and controlling pests.

Answer

124.
A. When the wax is removed, only the areas that were not waxed are coloured. **B.** The cloth is then dyed and dried. **C.** Instead of painting or printing a colour directly on a cloth, as in most patterned fabrics, the worker covers parts of the fabric with wax. **D.** The process used for batik is called resist dyeing.

Answer

125.
A. Friction comes from the Latin word meaning 'rub'. **B.** Friction always occurs when two articles are moved so as to rub or chafe against one another. **C.** This resistance, or force which opposes motion, is called friction. **D.** When a heavy wooden box is pushed along the floor, resistance is set up between the box and the floor.

Answer

126.
A. The eel-like hagfish has a very unpleasant way of life. **B.** Over 100 hagfish have been found in one large, dead fish. **C.** If the 'host' fish were alive originally, it slowly dies as its body is eaten away. **D.** It bores its way into the bodies of other fish – alive, dead or dying – and burrows through their flesh, eating as it goes.

Answer

127.
A. The laws were written in the Sumerian language, in wedge-shaped letters called cruciform. **B.** Hammurabi, a wise and able ruler, was concerned with bringing order and justice to his kingdom. **C.** This was a collection of more than 280 laws, which he had inscribed on a great stone pillar. **D.** He set up a strong central government and gathered all the laws of his kingdom into a great code.

Answer

128.
A. (Australia, though larger, is not usually counted as an island.) **B.** More than four-fifths of its area consists of a vast ice cap rising very gradually to a central dome, and only in the coastal regions can people live or plants grow. **C.** Greenland is about 2,670 km from north to south, and over 1,050 km at its widest point east to west. **D.** Greenland is the world's largest island and is located in the north Atlantic ocean, off the east coast of Canada.

Answer

129.
A. A standard medicine such as paracetamol (acetaminophen) may help to lower or relieve aches and pains, though it won't alter the course of the illness. **B.** Whooping cough and some of the other infections are caused by bacteria, in which case drugs may often help to fight the illness. **C.** Chickenpox, measles, German measles and mumps are all caused by viruses. **D.** Few drugs are effective against viruses, so the best treatment is to let the patient rest, as his or her body attacks and kills the viruses naturally.

Answer

130.
A. With it, it is possible to build dams, foundations, tall slender bridges, high-rise buildings, and paved areas such as roads and airfield runways. **B.** Cement is used in one of several ways in nearly every building in the Western world, and hundreds of millions of tonnes of cement are used throughout the world every year. **C.** Cement is one of the most versatile binders known to man. **D.** It is also used in the manufacture of building blocks, roofing tiles, and even things as thin as roofing sheet.

Answer

131.
A. This is doubtful. **B.** Paintings made in the first half of the 18th century show the members of one clan in different tartans, and even one clansman with separate tartans for his coat, waistcoat and kilt, and it is unlikely that the clans kept strictly to particular tartans until the 19th century. **C.** The oldest known painting showing Highland dress dates from about 1660, and few earlier records are reliable. **D.** It is sometimes claimed that the different Scottish tartans served in ancient times to distinguish not only the different clans but also the ranks of the clansmen.

Answer

132.

A. The body of the common African civet is about 90 cm long, a little less than the length of its bushy tail. B. The coarse grey fur is tinged with yellow and marked with black spots and bands. C. As a rule the civet lives in a hole in the ground, coming out mostly at night to search for rodents, birds and insects; it will also eat fruit. D. The civets of India and other parts of Asia, of which there are several kinds, are usually smaller and their fur is striped rather than spotted.

Answer

133.

A. Nowadays, many people camp without 'roughing it', using caravans, campers or tents with all the modern comforts of home: a cooker, shower, toilet and even a television. B. Tents have been used by people for thousands of years. C. Explorers and mountain climbers have camped in some of the most remote and unfriendly places on earth. D. They are still the chief homes for some, such as the wandering Bedouin of North Africa and Arabia.

Answer

134.

A. Slow-speed film (50 ASA or less) reacts slowly to light and is used in very bright conditions, such as sun or snow. B. Film comes in different 'speeds', given on the packet in ASA/ISO or DIN numbers. C. The light passing through the lens of a camera acts on the light-sensitive chemicals in the film which, after being developed (or processed), produces a negative from which prints can be made. D. Medium-speed film (50 to 125 ASA) is for normal sunny conditions, and fast-speed film (200 to 400 ASA) is best for cloudy or dim conditions.

Answer

135.
A. The state has been made habitable by water, natural gas and hydroelectric power, mostly brought in from the outside, and by the invention of air conditioning. **B.** Most of its landscape consists of rugged mountains, arid desert, mesas and buttes. **C.** More than 300 ranges of mountains cross the state north to south. **D.** Nevada is the driest state in the United States and one of the hottest.

Answer [ ]

136.
A. At intervals along the mycelium, fruiting bodies, or sporophores, develop. **B.** Mushrooms spread by spores that develop on the gills. **C.** These grow into a massive network of underground threads (mycelium). **D.** When the spores ripen they are released, and if they land in a warm, moist place they grow into thread-like chains of cells (hyphae).

Answer [ ]

137.
A. Some people are born with greater possibilities or 'potential intelligence' than others. **B.** Intelligence is improved by learning. **C.** It is no longer thought that intelligence is a general quality, underlying all behaviour and inherited wholly from our parents. **D.** However, this potential may not develop unless it is encouraged and stimulated by influences surrounding the child from birth.

Answer [ ]

138.
A. This usually amounts to about £16,000. B. Even so, some former MPs struggle to make ends meet. C. On top of this, they receive a 'winding-up' allowance to take care of any unpaid staff, and research or other expenses. D. MPs get golden handshakes and they are fairly generous, with payments of between 50 and 100 per cent of their annual £55,118 salary given to them when the electorate turns nasty.

Answer

139.
A. These include, for example, the use of diamonds in a dentist's drill. B. The remainder are used for industrial purposes, that is for useful as distinct from decorative purposes. C. Other applications of industrial diamonds are found in engineering, where tools with very hard surfaces are needed for cutting and grinding other hard surfaces. D. Less than 50 per cent of rough diamonds are suitable for cutting and turning into jewellery.

Answer

140.
A. Slowly, differences in ways of speaking become more and more marked, and these differences will eventually make a new dialect. B. Dialects come about when people who have been living together and speaking to one another in the same way move apart. C. Language changes, even as it is passed on from parents to children. D. Separation of groups of people by a move across a physical barrier, such as a mountain or a river, can lead to different ways of speaking the same language.

Answer

141.
A. The amount of work performed to bring about an energy change is exactly equal to the quantity of energy being converted into new forms. **B.** The total energy at the end of any change is the same as the total energy before the change. **C.** This is an important principle known as the conservation of energy. **D.** Energy may be changed from one form to another, and work is the process that brings about the change.

Answer

142.
A. Many of them reproduce so slowly that they are unable to make up for the numbers that are wiped out. **B.** It is thought that one species becomes extinct every day, while many more become threatened. **C.** Biologists estimate that 1 in 10 of all species is in danger of dying out. **D.** That means there are at least a million endangered species of plants and animals.

Answer

143.
A. Sometimes they are based on time – the worker being paid at a rate of so much an hour or so much a week; and sometimes they are based on articles produced – a shirt maker, for example, being paid at a rate of so much for every shirt made (piece work). **B.** Payments of this type are usually controlled by law, so that the worker is protected against a bad employer who might try to pay all or nearly all the wages in kind. **C.** Wages, or salaries, are payments by employers to their employees in return for work. **D.** Wages are paid in money, but sometimes they include payments in kind, as when a caretaker is provided with a rent-free house and miners are given free or very cheap coal.

Answer

144.
A. Throughout the world, techniques to measure pupil development and achievement have improved in recent years. B. Standardized tests are used to a great extent. C. These serve not only to compare a student with his or her fellow classmates but also to compare him or her with other students in the country at large. D. The emphasis on individual differences and pupil interests has led to better methods of assessment.

Answer

145.
A. This is known as the circular flow of income. B. In economic life people are dependent on each other. C. Whenever somebody spends, somebody else earns. D. Macroeconomics is the study of how the whole of a country's economy works.

Answer

146.
A. In fact the word 'echinoderm' means 'spiny-skinned'. B. In sea urchins this is very obvious. C. In many echinoderms these plates have knobs or spines on them that stick through the skin and give the creature a prickly appearance. D. The skeleton is made of hard, chalky plates just under the skin.

Answer

147.
A. The oceanic crust is only 6–8 km thick. B. There are two kinds of crust. C. The continental crust averages 35 km, but reaches a thickness of 60–70 km under high mountain ranges. D. One kind, the oceanic crust, is beneath the oceans and seas, while the other, the continental crust, composes the continents.

Answer

148.
A. Sound waves can neither be seen nor be felt, but the ear is so delicate that it catches all the shades of difference in them. **B.** Only when they reach the brain do we hear anything. **C.** The hammer, anvil and stirrup of the middle ear take up the vibrations, magnify them, and pass them on through the fluid of the cochlea to the nerve endings of the inner ear and so to the brain. **D.** A sound is first caught by that part of the ear that is outside the head and is then sent down the canal to the eardrum, making it vibrate.

Answer [   ]

149.
A. Dyslexia tends to run in families, and is more common in males than females. **B.** Most dyslexics also have problems with spelling. **C.** People with dyslexia have trouble seeing the differences between words, and will often misread them. **D.** They may reverse the letters in a word, for example substituting 'saw' for 'was', or find substitutes for the printed word, so that 'hot' may be read as 'pot'.

Answer [   ]

150.
A. The men wore plain linen collars, jerkins and breeches, and had short hair (which earned them the nickname 'Roundheads'), while the women chose dark, plain dress styles. **B.** The Royalist side continued to wear elegant court satins, plumed hats and, even for men, long ringlet hair styles. **C.** An important development in the middle of the 17th century was that clothing became an obvious symbol of the religious and political differences that split England during the Civil War. **D.** The Parliamentary forces, who were Puritans, adopted very plain clothes.

Answer [   ]

100 English usage questions

Employers are keen on tests of English usage because they want to establish that a candidate can be trusted to produce competent written work. How you use English in business should be, well, business-like, and employers want employees to write letters and e-mails that are clear and to the point. Most will not care if, for example, some punctuation marks are omitted or the finer nuances of grammar are ignored, provided the intended meaning remains unaffected. They want the job done and are unlikely to object unless the errors are serious enough to undermine the confidence of colleagues or customers in the competence of the writer or, worse, damage the image of their organization. They are not usually interested to know if, for example, you use semi-colons correctly (or at all), but they may be reassured to know that you can identify the correct application of the comma, colon and apostrophe.

Few employers' tests of English usage can be described as advanced. They mostly comprise questions at the intermediate level. The majority of candidates will quite quickly be able to revise the rules of usage sufficiently well to pass these tests. Even candidates who have long forgotten the grammar lessons of school or remember them with considerable dread can with sufficient practice master these tests. Once you have revised or learned the rules of usage, these tests will seem far more straightforward.

So, practise to revise the rules and you will better realize the principle behind the questions and recognize the significance of the possibly subtle differences between the suggested answers. You will then be well placed to attend on the day, fully prepared to press home your advantage.

Below you will find 100 practice questions presented in the two most common styles of question found in real tests. No time limits are imposed, but if it better suits your circumstances then by all means impose your own time constraint and answer the questions under exam-type conditions. Answers and explanations are provided in Chapter 8.

You will find hundreds more practice questions in the Kogan Page testing titles: *The Ultimate Psychometric Test Book*, 2006, *How To Pass Graduate Psychometric Tests*, third edition, 2007, and *The Graduate Psychometric Test Workbook*, 2005.

Correctly complete the sentence

This style of question requires that you select a pair of words from the suggested answers that correctly completes the sentence. You then record the letter that identifies that pair of words in the answer box.

This style of English usage question was once very common; it is now less popular but still in use. Even if you do not face this style of question it is still worth working through them as some important points of usage are revised.

1.   Hastings _____ developed as a holiday resort after _____ .

A
A seaside town
World War I

B
a seaside town,
the first world war

C
, a seaside town,
the First World War

D
, a Seaside Town,
World War I

                                    Answer [   ]

2.   When you attend the test centre be sure to bring your
      personal _____ test appointment _____ thinking cap.

A
ID, your
card and your

B
ID your
card, your

C
ID and your
card your

D
id, your
card plus your

                                    Answer [   ]

3.   In most tests taken on a computer be sure of your answer
      before submitting _____ _____ go back and review your
      answer.

A
It, you
Cannot

B
it you
can

C
it you,
can

D
it because you
cannot

                                    Answer [   ]

4.   The colon is most commonly used to introduce a list: _____

_____ .

A	B
Paul, John and David took pens, paper and pencils	Pens, paper and pencils were all that Paul, John and David took

C	D
Paul, John and David took Pens, Paper and Pencils	pens, paper and pencils were all that paul, john and david took

Answer [   ]

5.   The reason the environmental campaigner dropped his objection to nuclear _____ recognized that renewable alternatives _____ yet viable.

A	B	C	D
power, he	power he	power: he	power: he
where not	were not	were not	where not

Answer [   ]

6.   The head _____ was very surprised to see the _____ in the kitchen.

A	B	C	D
chief	chef	chief	chef
house fly	housefly	house-fly	house fly

Answer [   ]

7.   The event was _____ and the venue less than _____ full.

A	B	C	D
ill-timed	ill timed	illtimed	ill-timed
three-quarters	three-quarters	three quarters	threequarters

Answer [   ]

8.   She lived on a very busy _____, Farlow _____, and hated the sound of the cars.

A	B	C	D
Road	Road	road	road
Road	road	road	Road

Answer [   ]

9.   After a good _____ work Peter went to the gym and then for a shower in the _____ club.

A	B	C	D
day	day's	days'	days
employee's	employees'	employees	employee

Answer [   ]

10.   We will have lunch in _____ hour; do you think you will want _____ slice of pizza or two?

A	B	C	D
an	an	a	a
a	one	one	an

Answer [   ]

11. They spent _____ month of June in the French town and the sun shone almost _____ day.

A	B	C	D
the whole	all	all the	the all
every	each	every	each

Answer [   ]

12. We were hunting for _____ mushrooms but it was so dark in the wood that we could barely see _____.

A	B	C	D
some	any	[no word]	some
[no word]	something	anything	some

Answer [   ]

13. _____ asked everyone and still haven't discovered _____ cat it is.

A	B	C	D
They've	They're	They'll	There's
whose	who's	whose	who's

Answer [   ]

14. The food and drinks manufacturer announced that additives _____ would no longer be _____ in any of its products.

A	B	C	D
, including monosodium glutamate including	including monosodium glutamate included	including monosodium glutamate including	, including monosodium glutamate, included

Answer [   ]

15. An object that reflects all parts of the light spectrum except red looks _____ object that reflects all _____ light looks white.

A	B	C	D
red, an	red while an	red an	red, object
wavelength	wavelength	wavelengths	wavelengths

Answer [   ]

16. The painting has taken _____ weeks to complete but this is a lot _____ the last time it was done.

A	B	C	D
less	quite a few	quite a few	less
less than	fewer than	less than	fewer than

Answer [   ]

17. The exchange rate _____ the deal was done was not advantageous and consequently the product was not purchased by members of the social-economic group _____ it was promoted.

A	B	C	D
at which	of which	at what	at that
to whom	at which	to who	among whom

Answer [   ]

18. I asked Jim if he was going to the _____ you planning to _____

A	B	C	D
film? Are	film, are	film? Are	film. Are
go?	go.	go.	go?

Answer [   ]

19.   The newspaper made the _____ that it was a _____.

A	B	C	D
pre-sumption	presumption	pre-sumption	presumption
self portrait	self portrait	self-portrait	self-portrait

Answer [   ]

20.   Look at these artichokes: they are the best _____ I've seen but this _____ tastes rather bitter.

A	B	C	D
one	ones	[no word]	[no word]
[no word]	ones	one	[no word]

Answer [   ]

21.   The statement from the solicitor was _____ incomprehensible and made the judge _____ angry.

A	B	C	D
utterly	a bit	very	extremely
dreadfully	totally	nearly	completely

Answer [   ]

22.   The delay was _____ the large number of vehicles and perhaps another factor was _____ the road works.

A	B	C	D
owing to	because of	due to	because of
[no word]	owing to	[no word]	due to

Answer [   ]

23. _____ he was the cleverest in the family _____ at university he failed the most exams.

A	B	C	D
While	Even if	Although	Where as
Even if	while	whilst	though

Answer [ ]

24. By the time the administrator realized her estimate of the _____ of delegates was wrong it _____ too late.

A	B	C	D
number	amount	number	amount
was	would have been	will have been	will be

Answer [ ]

25. The _____ complained that the _____ sewing was of poor quality.

A	B	C	D
bosses'	bosss	bosses	boss's
seamstress	seamstresss'	seamstress's	seamstres's

Answer [ ]

26. He worked hard to improve his _____ in Italian but to hear him speak you would not think he _____ .

A	B	C	D
proficiently	proficiency	proficiently	proficiency
did	did	had	had

Answer [ ]

27. He got up early _____ walk the dog and left the house quietly _____ not to wake anyone.

A	B	C	D
in order to	to	so to	so as to
in such as way	so as	so	so that

Answer [   ]

28. The problem with the film is that the viewer is _____ provided with all the facts _____ told why they should expect events to unfold as they do.

A	B	C	D
either	neither	either	neither
nor	or	or	nor

Answer [   ]

29. Everyone knew the issue was of great _____ importance and the decision would set _____ important precedent.

A	B	C	D
[no word]	an	a	the
an	a	[no word]	the

Answer [   ]

30. I thought _____ left the keys in the car but realized this was something I _____ normally do.

A	B	C	D
its	I'd	I've	I'm
won't	wouldn't	who's	weren't

Answer [   ]

31. Half the team gave the proposal their _____ support while the rest thought it a _____ .

A	B	C	D
Un-conditional	unconditional	un-conditional	unconditional
nonstarter	nonstarter	nonstarter	non-starter

Answer [   ]

32. As soon as she finishes her _____ assignment she will be let _____ on the next one.

A	B	C	D
last	latest	late	later
lose	loose	lose	loose

Answer [   ]

33. I don't expect to get it back and only placed the advert in the lost and found section of the newspaper as a matter of _____ but if anyone calls about the lost money please _____.

A
principal
ask their number
and I will call back

B
moral correctness
ask them to call back

C
principal
ask that they
call back

D
principle
take a
number and I will call back

Answer [   ]

34. Here is the site of the laboratory _____ it was invented and
    it was over there _____ the discovery was put to its current
    day practical application.

A	B	C	D
when	whereby	where	whose
whose	where	whereby	when

Answer [   ]

35. I've always had an admiration _____ the work of Willard
    Van Orman Quine and share with him an interest _____
    travel

A	B	C	D
for	in	in	for
in	with	with	for

Answer [   ]

36. The incidence of heart disease _____ positively _____ the
    level of salt ingested.

A	B	C	D
correlate	correlates	correlate	correlates
with	to	to	with

Answer [   ]

37. The parliamentary session ended with the Prime Minister
    refusing to answer the _____ was responsible for the release
    of confidential _____

A	B	C	D
question of	question	question	who
who	who		
information.	information?	information.	information?

Answer [   ]

38. I _____ get the message because it arrived _____ I had left for the meeting.

A	B	C	D
did	did'nt	did not	didn't
no sooner	until	after	before

Answer [   ]

39. She told us '_____ favourite was _____ sausages'.

A	B	C	D
that my	My	my	my
Frankfurt	Frankfurt	frankfurt	Frankfurt

Answer [   ]

40. _____ sound broke the silence of the early morning and _____ felt like speaking for fear of breaking the magic of the moment.

A	B	C	D
No	Not a	Not any	None
no one	not any of them	not anyone	nothing

Answer [   ]

Identify the correct sentence

The following have been the predominant style of English usage questions. You are required to identify the correct sentence from a series of suggested answers and record in the answer box the letter of the alphabet that corresponds to your selected answer.

41.
A. She loved to travel so she could know people from all around the world.
B. She loved to travel so she could get to know people from round the world.
C. She loved to travel so she could knew about people from around the world.
D. She loved to travel so she could get knowing people from round the world.

Answer [   ]

42.
A. If it were not for the Prussians Wellington would have lost the battle at Waterloo.
B. If it hadn't been for the Prussians Wellington would have lost the battle at Waterloo.
C. But for the Prussians Wellington would have been lost at Waterloo.
D. If it wasn't for the Prussians Wellington would have lost at Waterloo.

Answer [   ]

43.

A. I felt like a drink but I was put off by the male feel of the bar.

B. I wanted a drink but I was put off by the masculine bar.

C. I felt like a drink but I was put off because the bar felt too masculine.

D. I wanted a drink but I was put off by the male bar.

Answer [   ]

44.

A. I kept explaining that Oxford is farther than Brighton but she kept asking for further information.

B. I kept explaining that Oxford is farther than Brighton but she kept asking for farther information.

C. I kept explaining that Oxford is further than Brighton but she kept asking for farther information.

D. I walked to the college of farther information but it was further away than I realized.

Answer [   ]

45.

A. The ocean depths being recognized as a featureless abyss rather than a dynamic variable and biologically rich environment.

B. By recognizing the ocean depths as dynamic, variable and biologically rich environment rather than a featureless abyss.

C. Their recognizing of the ocean depths as a featureless abyss rather than a dynamic, variable and biologically rich environment.

D. The ocean depths are recognized as a dynamic, variable and biologically rich environment.

Answer [   ]

46.
A. Thank you for bringing me here but let's look at one more picture and then would you please take me home.
B. Thanks for bringing me here but let's look at one more picture and then would you please bring me home.
C. Thank you for taking me here but let's look at one more picture and then would you please bring me home.
D. Thanks for taking me here but let's look at one more picture and then would you please bring me home.

Answer [   ]

47.
A. As soon as he suggested a weekend away she flew up the passage, jumped in the car and sped off down to the country.
B. As soon as he suggested a weekend away she flew up the passage, jumped in the car and sped off up to the country.
C. As soon as he suggested a weekend away she flew down the passage, jumped in the car and sped off down to the country.
D. As soon as he suggested a weekend away she flew down the passage, jumped in the car and sped off up to the country.

Answer [   ]

48.
A. When fishing you can always tell when you lose a fish because the line feels loose.
B. When fishing you can always tell when you loose a fish because the line feels lose.
C. When fishing you can always tell when you loose a fish because the line feels loose.
D. When fishing you can always tell when you lose a fish because the line feels lose.

Answer [   ]

49.
A. The milk tasted off and I meant to say something but I did not think of complaining.
B. The milk tasted off and I meant to complain but did not think to say something.
C. The milk tasted off and I meant to complain but decided its not worth it.
D. The milk tasted off and I meant to say something but did not think it worth complaining.

Answer [   ]

50.   Which of the following sentences draws a metaphor?
A. Karl Marx labelled the capitalist a parasite on the back of labour because the whole value or produce created by the labouring man belonged to the capitalist.
B. John Locke described how he who gathered the wild fruit, killed, caught or tamed the wild beasts by placing his labour on them acquired a property in them.
C. Adam Smith held that the original state of things which preceded both the appropriation of land and the accumulation of stock were held in common.
D. Galbraith argued for a better balance between private affluence and public poverty, including measures to protect the environment against the excesses of private companies.

Answer [   ]

51.
A. I willingly accepted to walk with them over the forest.
B. I reluctantly agreed to walk with them across the forest.
C. With hesitation I agreed to walk with them through the forest.
D. Despite misgivings I accepted to walk with them through the forest.

Answer [   ]

52.
A. In the restaurant where I work I get often tips because I always treat well the customers.
B. In the restaurant where I work I get often tips because I always treat the customers well.
C. In the restaurant where I work I often get tips because I always treat well the customers.
D. In the restaurant where I work I often get tips because I always treat the customers well.

Answer

53.
A. When she asked to borrow my computer, I replied yes I'm afraid so.
B. When she asked to borrow my computer, I replied I'm afraid so.
C. When she asked to borrow my computer, I replied I'm afraid not.
D. When she asked to borrow my computer, I replied I'm afraid no.

Answer

54.
A. He had nothing except what he was borne with.
B. He had nothing apart from what he was born with.
C. He had nothing besides what he was borne with.
D. He had nothing apart from what he was borne with.

Answer

55.

A. When the company went bust everyone involved lost all that they had.

B. When the company went bust everyone involved lost all.

C. When the company went bust everyone involved lost all what they had.

D. When the company went bust everyone involved lost what they had.

Answer [   ]

56.

A. After the garage sale the children hadn't hardly any toys left.

B. After the garage sale the children had scarcely any toys left.

C. After the garage sail the children had hardly any toys left.

D. After the garage sale the children hadn't scarcely any toys left.

Answer [   ]

57.

A. I lent my bother's car so I could go for a nice drive.

B. I borrow my brother's car so I could for a really nice drive.

C. I lend my brother's car so I could go for the drive of my life.

D. I borrowed my brother's car and all I did was sit in a traffic jam.

Answer [   ]

58.

A. My eldest daughter was born at 3 o'clock in the afternoon in a cold day in November.

B. My eldest daughter was born at 3 o'clock in the afternoon on a cold day in November.

C. My eldest daughter was born on exactly 3 o'clock in the afternoon in November.

D. My eldest daughter was born on the weekend at 3 o'clock in the afternoon.

Answer [   ]

59.   Which statement has a sarcastic tone?

A. After 20 years the moratorium on hunting whales remains riddled with loopholes that allow whales to be killed and their meat sold as food in the name of science.

B. For many successes there is usually an associated failure. For example, lots of couples rejoice in the fact that their house is worth much more than they paid for it, but they complain that their children can't afford the deposit to buy a home of their own.

C. It is time for religious believers to stand up to secularisms and to defend their faith against progressive policies.

D. He viewed all civil servants as at worst meddling bureaucrats and at best as pointless paper-shufflers.

Answer

60.

A. That particular species of fish is found across the world's oceans and you can identify it from its large colourful spots.

B. That particular species of fish is found over the world's oceans and you can identify it from it's large colourful spots.

C. That particular species of fish is found throughout the world's oceans and you can identify it from its large colour spots.

D. That particular species of fish is found beneath all the world's oceans and you can identify it from it's large colourful spots.

Answer

61.

A. As one gets older one better appreciates life's little comforts.

B. As you gets older one better appreciates life's little comforts.

C. As one gets older you better appreciates life's little comforts.

D. As you gets older you better appreciates life's little comforts.

Answer

62.
A. The police hoped for help in finding the culprit and the missing money from everyone.
B. The police hoped for help from everyone in finding the culprit and the missing money.
C. From everyone the police hoped for help in finding the culprit and the missing money.
D. The police hoped for help in finding the culprit from everyone and the missing money.

Answer [   ]

63.
A. Most professional athletes choose this kind of trainers.
B. Most professional athletes choose these kind of trainer.
C. Most professional athletes choose this kind of trainer.
D. Most professional athletes choose these kind of trainers.

Answer [   ]

64.
A. He lay between the sheets staring up at the ceiling.
B. He lie between the sheets staring up at the ceiling.
C. He lay among the sheets staring up at the ceiling.
D. He lie among the sheets staring up at the ceiling.

Answer [   ]

65.
A. Neither the right wing party or the left wing party is willing to concede defeat.
B. Neither the right wing party or the left wing party am willing to concede defeat.
C. Neither the right wing party nor the left wing party am willing to concede defeat.
D. Neither the right wing party nor the left wing party is willing to concede defeat.

Answer [   ]

66.

A. The research found that either obese children must take more exercise or eat less.

B. The research found that obese children must either take more exercise or eat less.

C. The research found that obese children either must take more exercise or eat less.

D. The research found that obese children must take either more exercise or eat less.

Answer [ ]

67.

A. The papers was requested at the same time as the request was made for the newspaper cuttings.

B. The papers were requested at the same time as the request were made for the newspaper cuttings.

C. The papers was requested at the same time as the request were made for the newspaper cuttings.

D. The papers were requested at the same time as the request was made for the newspaper cuttings.

Answer [ ]

68.

A. Over the years the trade federation has served its members well.

B. Over the years the trade federation have served it members well.

C. Over the years the trade federation has served their members well.

D. Over the years the trade federation have served its members well.

Answer [ ]

69.
A. Surprisingly, given the recent profits warning, the chief executive has enjoyed considerable support from they who had previously challenged his leadership.
B. Surprisingly, given the recent profits warning, the chief executive has enjoyed considerable support from them who had previously challenged his leadership.
C. Surprisingly, given the recent profits warning, the chief executive has enjoyed considerable support from he who had previously challenged his leadership.
D. Surprisingly, given the recent profits warning, the chief executive has enjoyed considerable support from those who had previously challenged his leadership.

Answer

70.
A. The fact that the number of humpback whales are increasing prove that the conservation efforts are effective.
B. The fact that the number of humpback whales are increasing proves that the conservation efforts are effective.
C. The fact that the number of humpback whales is increasing proves that the conservation efforts are effective.
D. The fact that the number of humpback whales is increasing prove that the conservation efforts are effective.

Answer

71.
A. If they had not taken so long checking each question before attempting the next question they might not have run out of time.
B. If they had taken so long checking each question before attempting the next question they might not have run out of time.
C. If they had not took so long checking each question before attempting the next question they might not have run out of time.
D. If they had took so long checking each question before attempting the next question they might not have run out of time.

Answer

72.
A. The firm is a major player in the logistics industry to play a significant role in keeping our supermarket shelves well stocked.
B. The firm is a major player in the logistics industry so it plays a significant role in keeping our supermarket shelves well stocked.
C. The firm is a major player in the logistics industry with it playing a significant role in keeping our supermarket shelves well stocked.
D. The firm is a major player in the logistics industry because it plays a significant role in keeping our supermarket shelves well stocked.

Answer ☐

73.
A. I might have paid greater tribute to the contribution of his research assistant had I made the speech at the awards ceremony.
B. I might have paid greater tribute to the contribution of his research assistant if I make the speech at the awards ceremony.
C. I might have paid greater tribute to the contribution of his research assistant if I am making the speech at the awards ceremony.
D. I might have paid greater tribute to the contribution of his research assistant making the speech at the awards ceremony.

Answer ☐

74.
A. The food was cooked to perfection but the portions were too small, also we waited too long between the courses as well.
B. The food was cooked to perfection but the portions were too small and as well we waited too long between the courses.
C. The food was too well cooked and the portions too small, also we waited too long between the courses.
D. The food was over cooked, the portions were small and we waited a long time between the courses too.

Answer [   ]

75.
A. The amount of drivers of Ford cars who responded to the survey is as high as it's ever been.
B. The number of drivers of Ford cars who responded to the survey is as high that it's ever been.
C. The amount of drivers of Ford cars who responded to the survey is as high that it's ever been.
D. The number of drivers of Ford cars who responded to the survey is as high as it's ever been.

Answer [   ]

76.
A. The class concluded that the exam question was very impossible.
B. The assignment is not very possible.
C. The project was quite impossible.
D. It is widely known that the puzzle is fairly impossible to solve.

Answer [   ]

77.   Which sentence includes an example of personification?

A. Nomadic people are the human equivalent of an endangered species and have no defence against the encroachment of loggers and ranchers onto their ancestral lands.

B. Take airline pilots for example; they do not need to attend university to qualify for this job and most pilots are on a salary of $150,000 or more.

C. Recent research provided further stark evidence that in education money still talks, when it was found that bright children from poor homes are failing to get the same grades as bright children from rich households.

D. Planning and then recording in a last will and testament how we would wish our assets dealt with on our death is something more of us should do, and for the majority of us with straight-forward affairs a 'do it yourself' will would suffice.

Answer [   ]

78.

A. By the time they had completed checking all the forms it will be time to start double-checking them.

B. By the time they had completed checking all the forms it will have been time to start the double-check.

C. By the time they had completed checking all the forms it was time to start the double-check of them.

D. By the time they had completed checking all the forms it was time to start double-checking them.

Answer [   ]

79.
A. The girls come to stay alternate weekends and it is so nice to have the family all together.
B. The girls come to stay alternative weekends and it's so nice to have the family all together.
C. The girls come to stay alternative weekends and it is so nice to have the family altogether.
D. The girls come to stay alternate weekends and it is so nice to have the family altogether.

Answer

80.
A. I met a new acquaintance at the club today.
B. I made a new acquaintance at the club today.
C. I meet a new acquaintance at the club today.
D. I came to a new acquaintance at the club today.

Answer

81.
A. Try and eat bread and butter with a fork and knife and you will probably end up on your hands and knees picking it up off the floor.
B. If you try and eat bread and butter with a knife and fork you are bound to end up on your knees and hands picking it up off the floor.
C. If you have ever eaten butter and bread with a knife and fork I expect you ended up on your hands and knees picking your food up from the floor.
D. If you try to eat bread and butter with a knife and fork you are very likely to end up on your hands and knees picking it up off the floor.

Answer

82.
A. Overall the price increase had the effect of reinforcing the committee members in their determination to increase interest rates.
B. Overall the price increase had the affect of reinforcing the committee members in its determination to increase interest rates.
C. Overall the price increase had the affect of reinforcing the committee members in their determination to increase interest rates.
D. Overall the price increase had the effect of reinforcing the committee members in its determination to increase interest rates.

Answer

83. Which sentence suffers most from hyperbole?
A. Most collectors of postage stamps would give the Earth to own one of the 1920s 24-cent US stamps with an upside-down biplane.
B. It used to be thought that a diet high in fibre greatly reduced the risk of cancer but it is now thought that eating too much red meat and milk products have a much stronger negative association.
C. There have been many fabulously successful public relations campaigns but when things go wrong they can go spectacularly wrong.
D. We face a pensions crisis because more than half of all working people will rely solely on the state to provide a pension in their old age and the state cannot be trusted to pay it.

Answer

84.

A. As the train moved away from the track the passengers started to jump into the station platform.

B. As the train moved on the track the passengers jumped out of the station platform.

C. As the train moved with the track the passengers jumped out of the station platform.

D. As the train moved along the track the passengers started to jump off on to the station platform.

Answer [   ]

85.   Which of the following can you correctly describe as cynical in tone?

A. He wrote saying that he wants to enter the priesthood but I very much doubt that he is serious.

B. The charity raises money to help the homeless but the people working there seem most interested in helping themselves.

C. The election result is a great disappointment.

D. Can you believe it that Frank is going to get married again!

Answer [   ]

86.

A. No whales were seen the whole month but ask some expert and they will tell you that they will turn up any time.

B. Not any whales were seen the whole month but ask any expert and they will tell you they will turn up some time.

C. No whales were seen the whole month but ask any expert and they will tell you that they will turn up some time.

D. Not any whales were seen the whole month but ask some expert and they will tell you they could turn up any time.

Answer [   ]

87.

A. Mother suggested that the children bring their instruments into the front room but still they played the violins like they were trying to saw them in half.

B. Mother suggested the children bring their instruments in the front room but still they played the violins as if they were trying to saw them in half.

C. Mother suggested the children bring their instruments in the front room but still they played the violins like they were trying to saw them in half.

D. Mother suggested the children bring their instruments into the front room but still they played the violins as if they were trying to saw them in half.

Answer

88.   Which sentence includes a euphemism?

A. He is difficult to understand when he speaks in that childish voice.

B. I was really surprised to find out that our house was built over 100 years ago

C. A cemetery is a place where people are buried when they pass away.

D. It is stupid to get annoyed about things that do not really matter.

Answer

89.

A. Foggy though it was the sun still managed to shine through.

B. Foggy as though it was the sun still managed to shine through.

C. Although it was foggy the sun still managed to shine though.

D. Foggy through it was the sun still managed to shine though.

Answer

90.
A. The collected datum is proving its possible after all.
B. The collected datum is proving it's possible after all.
C. The collected datum are proving it's possible after all.
D. The collected datum are proving its possible after all.

Answer

91. In which of the following does the verb directly transmit action from the subject to the object?
A. These days the world is run by computers.
B. The world would be a very different place if it were not for computers.
C. A world without computers would be a better place.
D. These days computers run the world.

Answer

92.
A. If it would have rained on the last day of the month it would have been the wettest July on record.
B. If it would had rained on the last day of the month it would have been the wettest July on record.
C. Would have it rained on the last day of the month it would have been the wettest July on record.
D. Had it rained on the last day of the month it would have been the wettest July on record.

Answer

93.
A. Anyone interested in the reptiles found in Sardinia can learn much if you search on the internet.
B. Anyone interested in the reptiles found in Sardinia can learn much by searches on the internet.
C. Anyone interested in the reptiles found in Sardinia can learn much if they search on the internet.
D. Anyone interested in reptiles found in Sardinia can learn much if she searches on the internet.

Answer

94. Which of the following statements includes a simile?
A. A red, white and blue flag fluttered.
B. He wandered as if he had all the time in the world.
C. It was a lovely sunny day until the fog rolled in.
D. The shape of the hill was like a fairy cake.

Answer [   ]

95.
A. The newspaper reported the football coach as saying that hopefully his team would win.
B. The newspaper reported the football coach as saying that he was full of hope his team would win.
C. The newspaper reported the football coach as saying that he hoped his team would win.
D. The newspaper reported the football coach as saying that he was full of hope his team should win.

Answer [   ]

96.
A. He is at a meeting at Newport, the town at the centre of the island.
B. He is in a meeting at Newport, the town in the centre of the island.
C. He is in a meeting at Newport, the town at the centre of the island.
D. He is at a meeting in Newport, the town at the centre of the island.

Answer [   ]

97.
A. First I thought I was the only undergraduate at the lecture besides Michele.
B. At first I thought I was the only undergraduate at the lecture beside Michele.
C. At first I thought I was the only undergraduate at the lecture besides Michele.
D. First I thought I was the only undergraduate at the lecture beside Michele.

Answer [   ]

98.
A. The criminal recidivist promised to try to change his ways.
B. The reoffending recidivist promised to try and change his ways.
C. The convicted recidivist promised to try to change his ways.
D. The recidivist promised to try and change his ways.

Answer [   ]

99. Which of the following contains a non-sequitur?
A. Most people do not have a sufficient grasp of statistics to tell whether or not the figures produced by their government are correct or being used correctly.
B. Public trust in official data is at an all time low and we can't insist that the general public go back to school and attend classes on the meaning of data and what can be correctly interpreted from it.
C. To produce the official annual inflation rate, government statisticians monitor the price of a basket of 650 goods and services sold at a total of 120,000 outlets.
D. No one can control how statistics are used. Imagine if some statistician were to be made judge in every debate and intervened to endorse or reject contesting interpretations put onto official figures.

Answer [   ]

100.
A. I might have offered the guests a complimentary cup of coffee if I had been the proprietor of that restaurant.
B. I might have offered the guests a complimentary cup of coffee if I had to be the proprietor of that restaurant.
C. I might have offered the guests a complimentary cup of coffee if I were the proprietor of that restaurant.
D. I might have offered the guests a complimentary cup of coffee if I was the proprietor of that restaurant.

Answer [   ]

100 True, false or cannot tell questions

This chapter contains 33 passages and 100 warm-up questions for what is fast becoming the most common type of verbal reasoning test question. You are bound to face these reading comprehension and critical reasoning questions at some stage in your career.

Each passage is following by three questions (the exception is the last passage which is followed by four). Your task is to answer the questions by referring to each passage. You must determine if the correct answer is true, false or that you cannot tell (ie you cannot tell from the information given if the answer is true or false). The questions require you, for example, to comprehend meaning and significance, assess logical strength, identify valid inference, distinguish between a main idea and a subordinate one, recognize the writer's intention and identify a valid summary, interpretation or conclusion.

The subjects of the passage are drawn from a great many fields. It may be current affairs, business, science, the environment, economics, history, meteorology, health or education. In fact, expect almost any subject matter. If you know something of the area then take care not to bring your own knowledge to the passage. You are expected to answer the questions using only the information it contains. Be especially careful if you know a great deal about the subject or if you believe the passage to be factually incorrect or controversial. It is not a test of your general knowledge, your knowledge of the latest findings in the discipline or your political views. So feel at ease about answering true to a statement that is true in the very limited context of the passage but which you know to be false given what you learned at university or read in a newspaper that morning.

When publishers of real tests develop an advanced verbal reasoning test they rely on fine distinctions between the suggested answers in order to distinguish between the scores of the large numbers of candidates. These distinctions are much finer than those we draw on a day-to-day basis. As a result it is common for candidates to feel irritation and complain that these tests are to a large extent arbitrary. In a way they are; after all, this is not how we use language at work or anywhere other than in the surreal world of tests. This is something you just have to accept and get used to and with practice you will get to recognize the subtle distinctions being drawn.

Take care not to err too much towards the 'cannot tell' answer by making the mistake of applying too strict or too inflexible a test of proof. Be sure to read the questions as carefully as you read the passage and learn to pick up the many clues provided in the wording. For example, if the passage refers to 'a valid argument, inference or premise', or asks whether it is necessarily the case that..., then apply a strict criterion of proof. However, if the question asks, for example, is it reasonable... on the balance of probability, that... might the author..., then adjust your criterion accordingly and apply a less strict one. Once again, the only way to master these subtle differences is to practise. You will soon gain more confidence and get better at making the proper judgements.

If, when taking lots of time in the relaxed conditions of your home, you find these questions easy, take care that you do not slip into a false sense of security. In a real test you will be pressed for time and may well be suffering some anxiety. You should aim to undertake just one careful read of the passage and then refer back to it to answer the question. Some people find it helps to read the questions before the passage.

You will find more practice questions at the advanced level in these Kogan Page test titles: *The Graduate Psychometric Workbook*, 2005, and *How to Pass Graduate Psychometric Tests*, third edition, 2007.

Passage 1

NASA, the US space agency, announced plans to return to the Moon within the next 15 years and this time the plan is to stay. It was 1972 when the last people stepped onto the moon. The next time an astronaut walks there he or she is most likely to visit the polar region rather than the equatorial zone, the site of all previous missions. The poles are the preferred location because they experience more moderate temperatures and are bathed in almost continuous sunlight, which will allow a permanent research station to rely on solar power. Another benefit of the poles regions is that they are believed to hold mineral deposits from which oxygen and hydrogen can be extracted. After a number of robotic scouting missions there would then occur a great many short-duration manned transportation missions. Once operational the station would be permanently occupied with astronauts undertaking six monthly tours of duty. They would undertake a wide range of scientific tasks perhaps the most ambitious of which will be to prepare for a journey to the planet Mars.

1. Incredibly, or more likely unintentionally, the passage states that the next astronaut will have to walk to the moon!

    True   False   Cannot tell

                                  Answer [   ]

2. The moon station will operate as a science laboratory and
    its principal objective will be preparing for a manned
    mission to Mars.

    True   False   Cannot tell

                                 Answer   [   ]

3. The conclusion that the polar region of the moon is the
    preferred location for the station is wholly dependent on the
    assumption that the oxygen and hydrogen extracted there
    could be used by the astronauts.

    True   False   Cannot tell

                                 Answer   [   ]

Passage 2

Outside the cities, people have no alternative but to drive their
cars to get their children to school, get to hospitals and to go
shopping. They already pay among the highest petrol duties in the
world and an annual road tax that raises far more than is spent on
the national infrastructure. Now they face, within a decade, the
introduction of road charging, an additional tax that will be
charged for each mile travelled. The aim of these additional taxes
is to free the roads of traffic, so speeding up businesses and
improving the nation's productivity and efficiency. Then the well
off will be able to drive along unencumbered by the mass of
ordinary drivers, and the congestion of the rush hour will be a
thing of the past.

4. A significant flaw in the case made in the passage would
    emerge if there were an affordable public transport system
    serving rural locations.

True   False   Cannot tell

Answer [   ]

5. People living outside the cities already pay a higher rate of duty on petrol than those living in the city.

True   False   Cannot tell

Answer [   ]

6. The rich will be able to drive along unencumbered by the mass of ordinary drivers only if the charges are so high that the majority of road users are priced off the roads.

True   False   Cannot tell

Answer [   ]

Passage 3

Cholera, typhoid, diphtheria and tuberculosis cause huge numbers of deaths. Drinking water has always been the world's greatest single vector of sickness. Disease is transmitted when sewage and drinking water come into contact. Children are particularly vulnerable. In the 19th century half of all children died before the age of 5. In some of the poorest countries the infant mortality rate still stands as high as one in eight. This compares with a rate of 1 in 100 in countries where drinking water is safe. The separation of sewage and the supply of clean drinking water are the domain of civil engineers, and their work makes a significant contribution to public health. That contribution was at last recognized when public sanitation was voted the greatest medical breakthrough, beating discoveries including antibiotics, vaccines and anaesthesia in a poll organized by the *British Medical Journal.*

7.   The passage states that cholera is a water-borne disease.

   True   False   Cannot tell

                                 Answer [   ]

8.   The safe disposal of sewage and the supply of clean drinking water are not medical advances.

   True   False   Cannot tell

                                 Answer [   ]

9.   The first two sentences are sufficient to draw the conclusion that water-borne disease is still the greatest transmitter of sickness.

   True   False   Cannot tell

                                 Answer [   ]

Passage 4

'End the external consultant's gravy train' was the message from the cross-party accounts committee of the Houses of Parliament. The use of consultants in the public sector has soared over the past three years to the point where members of the committee considered it to have reached an expensive, unproductive dependency. The evidence they heard left them unable to establish the benefit of the practice, and they voiced deep concerns about the lack of performance reviews in most contracts. They were also critical of the failure of management to support in-house tenders submitted by departments' own teams. The view of the committee was that these bids represented far greater value for money when compared to the companies that were awarded the work and who charged rates as high as £2,000 a day. It was also felt that savings could be made if, instead of payment on the time taken, consultants were engaged on price paid for the work done.

10. A gravy train is a situation where someone can easily make a lot of money.

   True   False   Cannot tell

                                 Answer

11. The passage states findings of an investigation by the committee into the benefits of using consultants in the private sector.

   True   False   Cannot tell

                                 Answer

12. Billions have been wasted on consultants over the three years.

   True   False   Cannot tell

                                 Answer

Passage 5

People should buy more fresh food to use in preparing proper meals. What is more, they should whenever possible buy locally produced food from local shops. Instead, we treat food like fuel: we seek out the cheapest and most convenient, which is often processed industrially and supplied by multinationals, which has consequences for both public health and the environment. We eat it in a hurry and on the move rather than eating together around a table. Many meals contain too much fat and sugar, giving rise to obesity and high blood pressure; pre-packed meals are expensive and wasteful because of all the packaging and distribution involved. People just do not respect food enough and largely lack the skills and knowledge needed to turn back to good food.

13.　The author's attitude towards junk food is ambivalent.

True　　　　　False　　　　　Cannot tell

Answer [   ]

14.　It can be inferred from the passage that pre-packed meals are cheaper than fresh food.

True　　　　　False　　　　　Cannot tell

Answer [   ]

15.　The author would probably consider the fact that people do not have time to appreciate food, buy it locally, prepare and cook it themselves and eat it together, as illustrative of his argument.

True　　　　　False　　　　　Cannot tell

Answer [   ]

Passage 6

Road signs and traffic lights at junctions and busy crossing points may be removed in order to improve road safety. The idea may seem contradictory and goes against the decades-long trend of separating and controlling traffic and pedestrians. The idea is to create anxiety, principally in the mind of the driver, so that he or she slows down and pays greater attention. Current demarcations between pavement and road will be made indistinct by removing railings and kerbs, resurfacing both in the same material, and re-laying them so that they are on the same level. Neither drivers nor pedestrians will then feel they have right of way and both, as a consequence, will behave more cautiously. When a driver reaches a junction at which there are no traffic lights he or she must take responsibility for deciding when it is safe to cross. Previously the driver relied on the traffic lights to decide his or her action and this created a dangerous state of denial of accountability. Incredibly, the initiative is claimed to not only make the streets safer but also to reduce congestion.

16. An explanation of the ultimate sentence in the passage would be 'Traffic moves more naturally and there are no more unnecessary delays at red lights when no other vehicle is in the vicinity.'

    True   False   Cannot tell

                                 Answer

17. If you observe a junction where the lights are out there is rarely congestion.

    True   False   Cannot tell

                                 Answer

18. The principal case made in the passage can be summed up as 'Removing lights removes barriers to traffic flow and improves behaviour.'

    True   False   Cannot tell

                                 Answer

Passage 7

Particles were collected in blocks of a silicon-type material called Aerogel as a space probe passed through the tail of a comet at the very edge of our solar system. Incredibly the probe then returned to Earth and scientists were able to use spectrometers and electron microscopes to identify the mineral and chemical compositions of the particles. The probe travelled almost 3 billion miles and passed within 150 miles of the comet at great speed. At that point the Aerogel was exposed and particles from the comet's tail that struck it were slowed down and stopped by the gel-like material, trapping them. The Aerogel and its unique cargo then began the three-year journey back to Earth. Some of the particles are believed to pre-date the sun and to have remained unchanged in very cold deep space for all of their existence. Importantly, the sample was considered free of contaminants derived from the great planets of our solar system and the asteroid belt.

19. Among the finds were particles that pre-dated our solar system that had not changed since their creation.

   True   False   Cannot tell

                                 Answer ⬚

20. According to the passage, the findings have startled scientists.

   True   False   Cannot tell

                                 Answer ⬚

21. The claim that the particles were too small to reveal their mineral content can be rebutted by the content of the passage.

   True   False   Cannot tell

                            Answer [   ]

Passage 8

A survey of how children spend their pocket money found that a sizable amount of it is spent on sweets, snacks and fizzy drinks. The study was based on 4,000 children who were asked to keep a diary of their purchases over a two-year period. On average the children spent $23 a week and over a third of this was spent on sugary and fatty food and drinks. The survey found marked differences in spending trends in sex and age. Boys spent less on clothes, shoes and toiletries and more on games, computer-related items and hobbies. The biggest spenders where children aged 13 to 15 years. The children spent equal sums on mobile phones and charges, and activities and objects that could be classed as educational. Both sexes spent equal amounts on music, but boys spent more on sporting activities.

22. The survey probably confirms many parents' worst fears.

   True   False   Cannot tell

                            Answer [   ]

23. The survey found that boys devote a greater part of their non-food spending on sporting activities than girls.

   True   False   Cannot tell

                            Answer [   ]

24. The passage does not allow the reader to infer the amount children spend on books.

True   False   Cannot tell

                                    Answer   [   ]

Passage 9

Workers now caught by the top rate of income tax include university lecturers, mid-ranking civil servants and officers of local authorities, specialist nurses and sisters, police inspectors and senior officers in the ambulance and fire service. This trend means that an extra 3.5 million workers are liable for the higher rate of tax compared to 10 years ago. More than 1 million extra people pay tax at the higher rate because growth in pay has increased faster than inflation-linked tax allowances. Over the period, these allowances have been increased in line with or less than inflation, while wages have increased at a rate of more than inflation. As a result, every year more people find themselves taxed at the highest rate for the first time. The Treasury defends the trend on the basis that the increase in numbers is a result of rising incomes and living standards. Critics point out that the higher rate of tax begins at a far lower point that in other countries. In Spain, the highest rate of tax is not applied until income is 2.5 times the average wage, while in the UK the highest rate is paid by anyone who earns 1.3 times the average wage.

25. The trend to which the passage refers is of wages increasing at a rate higher than inflation.

True   False   Cannot tell

                                    Answer   [   ]

26. Linking tax allowances to inflation has caused over 3 million people to pay the higher rate of tax.

    True   False   Cannot tell

                                 Answer

27. The cause of the increase can correctly be summarized as growth in pay having outstripped inflation-linked tax allowances, so the number of people paying tax at the highest rate has increased.

    True   False   Cannot tell

                                 Answer

Passage 10

Intellectual property is little more than the right to extract payment when our cultural outpourings should be free to share. In the digital world we are all authors, publishers and critics, so why should some be allowed to lay claim to our common cultural heritage and expression and enjoy the recognition of paternity? Why should the corporate media conglomerates be allowed to use copyright, patents and intellectual property laws to make criminals of thousands of users of virtual communities if they share music videos and written works? These users freely share their own work, and if all work were to be donated in this way the public sphere would be transformed into a more cultural, creative place.

28. The author of the passage would agree that the people who write books, poems, plays and film scripts, even through they may have taken years to write them, should donate the product of their craft for free.

    True   False   Cannot tell

                              Answer [   ]

29. The passage does not present an either/or scenario but allows for a balance to be struck.

    True   False   Cannot tell

                              Answer [   ]

30. The word 'paternity' in the context of the passage means 'fatherhood'.

    True   False   Cannot tell

                              Answer [   ]

Passage 11

Our international institutions and treaties have failed to move with the times. They were formed to provide mechanisms through which to confront common threats while protecting national interests. But interdependence and interconnectedness have advanced beyond anything imagined at that time and the global institutions have proved utterly impotent at providing effective global governance. On the one hand we have a fast emerging global economy and a spectrum of global communities but no effective global governance. All too often efforts to address the many common challenges are pulled down by narrow national interest. Collectively we have proved incapable of protecting the environment from the damage wreaked by individual companies and nations. Those institutions have proved powerless. The world lacks and increasingly needs mechanisms capable of protecting the collective.

31.   The author believes that the world needs a new system of global stewardship.

      True   False   Cannot tell

                                 Answer   [   ]

32.   It can be inferred from the passage that we are in the middle of a global revolution.

      True   False   Cannot tell

                                 Answer   [   ]

33.   The passage is correctly classified as an example of the liberal school of political thinking. This school of thought argues that the interests of the nation state must be protected and the individual must be protected from the excesses of government.

      True   False   Cannot tell

                                 Answer   [   ]

Passage 12

The Environmental Commissioner of the European Commission wants to introduce tough new limits for the omissions of carbon dioxide for all new vehicles. She wants mandatory maximum levels of emissions for all new cars by 2012. Manufacturers are lobbying against a mandatory limit and prefer a voluntary target for average emissions that is lowered annually, year on year. The luxury brand manufacturers are lobbying hardest, as they consider a mandatory limit to represent the greatest threat to their operations. The Industrial Commissioner has proposed a compromise that favours voluntary targets but will also commit manufacturers to realizing improvements in tyre performance, the introduction of emission-reducing speed management systems, and greener manufacturing and recycling of vehicles. European car makers believe that many jobs will be lost if the Environmental Commissioner gets her way. The 20 Commissioners who make up the Commission will have to decide.

34. The author sees the issue as a test of the Commission's green credentials.

    True   False   Cannot tell

                                  Answer

35. Members of the Commission are split over the decision.

    True   False   Cannot tell

                                  Answer

36. The passage contains a tautology.

    True   False   Cannot tell

                                  Answer

Passage 13

So many people ask why children aren't taught grammar and punctuation at school. Many of our teachers today have been produced by the same education system that they now teach in, so the simple answer is that they can't teach grammar and punctuation because they have never learnt it themselves. There have in recent years been meaningful improvements in the level of functional literacy among school leavers, but at the other end of the spectrum universities are complaining about the poor writing skills of undergraduates. These complaints are not raised because of a failure by students to correctly use the subjective clause or to err by leaving participles dangling, but far more fundamental failures in, for example, the use of apostrophes and capitalization. Most commentators describe errors of grammar and punctuation as irritating. To become irritated one must first recognize the error, and the majority of people, including many teachers, do not have a sufficient grasp of the rules to realize that a mistake has been made.

37. Most people don't object to bad grammar and punctuation.

   True   False   Cannot tell

                                 Answer

38. You can infer from the passage that you can only break a rule of grammar if you know the rule in the first place.

   True   False   Cannot tell

                                 Answer

39. The author would agree that bad grammar might be an irritant for a small number of purists but otherwise it does not matter.

True   False   Cannot tell

                                    Answer

Passage 14

El Niño, the cyclic warming of the Pacific Ocean, is largely responsible for the recent worldwide period of higher than average temperatures. February was the sixth warmest since records began in 1880, but January's record high means that the two-month period was the warmest worldwide. The averages were obtained by combining land and ocean surface temperatures. The only exceptions were areas of the Middle East and central areas of the United States, which did not experience record temperatures. Some of the largest temperature increases occurred in high latitudes around the Artic Circle, where wildlife has responded to the early spring-like weather. Should March not follow the trend and a wintry spell return, some of the species that have woken early from hibernation or started breeding prematurely may experience problems.

40. The passage can be correctly summarized as describing the world's two warmest winter months since records began.

True   False   Cannot tell

                                    Answer

41. China did not experience record temperatures.

True   False   Cannot tell

                                    Answer

42. If the average had been based only on land temperatures rather than land *and* ocean temperatures, the result would have been cooler.

   True   False   Cannot tell

                                 Answer

Passage 15

The Bank of England Monetary Policy Committee is discussing the next shift in interest rates. A month ago, every commentator would have predicted an increase, but since then two big trends have emerged, one international the other national, and no one now expects a rise. Instead the talk is of cuts, but for the time being anyway it is probably too early to say when a cut might be made. There has been a series of downbeat figures across the Eurozone. Italy and the Netherlands are officially in recession and manufacturing figures for Germany are in contraction. The French economy may be even weaker than generally perceived. As far as the UK is concerned, figures for the retail and housing sector suggest they have both slowed and demand for manufactured goods is following the global decline. Meanwhile, the price of services has risen above the level of inflation and in line with rising wage costs.

43. The international trend referred to in the passage relates to disappointing data from Europe.

   True   False   Cannot tell

                                 Answer

44. The national context has recently become one in which there is very little pressure for an interest rate rise.

     True   False   Cannot tell

                                  Answer   [   ]

45. It can be concluded from the passage that the Bank of England Monetary Policy Committee will cut interest rates soon.

     True   False   Cannot tell

                                  Answer   [   ]

Passage 16

Children as young as 4 will qualify for summer schools, Saturday morning school and online tuition under a scheme to track the brightest of children through school and on to university. The scheme is a major extension of the national gifted and talented agenda to address the fact that mixed-ability teaching has failed to challenge the brightest. 'Gifted' refers to children of high intelligence, while 'talented' is applied to children with an exceptional ability in a specific discipline. In every school a teacher will be made responsible for identifying beneficiaries and they will rely on their peers, assessments and national Key Stage tests. However, teachers tend to recommend children who produce good work on paper and who behave themselves rather than the really gifted and talented. This means that, for example, the child whose high intelligence makes him or her a bit of a misfit is overlooked.

46. Children not labelled as gifted may well feel like failures.

     True   False   Cannot tell

                                  Answer   [   ]

47. Gifted and talented children will be identified by their peers.

   True   False   Cannot tell

                                 Answer

48. A reason given for the initiative is that gifted or talented children may not always behave themselves.

   True   False   Cannot tell

                                 Answer

Passage 17

Scandinavia is an egalitarian delight if compared to Greece on the division of domestic labour between the sexes. Greek men were the least reconstructed in Europe, but almost as bad are the Czechs, where just 2 per cent of men admit to ironing their own clothes and only 5 per cent claim to do any cleaning in their homes. Men are slightly better represented in the kitchens of northern Europe, with one in five men claiming to be mainly responsible for cooking, but less than 10 per cent in the southern states. For cleaning their homes, the top men are from Latvia and Demark, who are twice as likely to clean as their Spanish counterparts.

49. An important flaw in the case made would emerge if it were discovered that women want equality at home as well as in work.

   True   False   Cannot tell

                                 Answer

50. The primary purpose of the passage is to promote equality of the sexes.

   True   False   Cannot tell

                                Answer [   ]

51. It is possible that women living in the south of Europe do not expect men to share responsibility for the family, while their northern counterparts do.

   True   False   Cannot tell

                                Answer [   ]

Passage 18

The hippocampus region of the brain usually starts to shrink when we reach the age of 30. This contraction is held to be responsible for age-related memory loss, and the older we get the worse it becomes. The process may be reversible though, as the hippocampus is the only region of the brain in which neurons can grow. New research suggests that the secret to growing them is physical exercise, which raises the possibility of us working out to boost our brain power. Unfortunately, it is not just any sort of exercise that stimulates the growth of neurons and this explains why physically active people suffer the same memory loss as the more sedentary.

52. Researchers have identified the forms of physical exercise that stimulate the growth of neurons in the hippocampus.

   True   False   Cannot tell

                                Answer [   ]

53. The intended audience of the passage is the physically inactive rather than the general population.

   True   False   Cannot tell

                                 Answer   [   ]

54. By saying that contraction of the hippocampus is held to be responsible, the author indicates that there may be disagreement on the point.

   True   False   Cannot tell

                                 Answer   [   ]

Passage 19

According to the 'best MBA annual survey', The Lynx Business School has been the best in the world for the last three years. Four of the best five schools are based in the United States; the fifth, based in Europe, is the Glasgow Business School. Stanford and Harvard were in second and third place respectively. In seventh place, up three from the last survey, came the University of the North West. Currently in nineteenth place is the Bombay School, the highest ranked business school outside of the United States and Europe.

55. The Lynx Business School is based in the United States.

   True   False   Cannot tell

                                 Answer   [   ]

56. The Glasgow Business School came fifth in the survey.

   True   False   Cannot tell

                                 Answer   [   ]

57. By 'best' the author of the survey most likely means the school voted by a panel of experts to be the pre-eminent.

True   False   Cannot tell

Answer

Passage 20

The number of very young children with diabetes has risen dramatically in the past 20 years. The number of children under 5 who have the type 1 form of the condition has increased fivefold. This dramatic increase is either the symptom of a marked improvement in diagnosis, or because more genetically suscep-tible children are surviving birth and infancy, or it suggests that the environment in which we raise our children has become more dangerous for their future health. The exact cause is unknown, but it is believed to be at least in part inherited. The chances of a child developing type 1 diabetes remains low, but the recent increase is too great to be explained by genetic factors alone. It may be that we are exposing our children to something new and that is the cause, or that we have reduced exposure to something that was preventing it previously.

58. It is reasonable to conclude from the passage that five times as many young children develop diabetes now than did 20 years ago.

True   False   Cannot tell

Answer

59. If the cause is environmental, then the author would agree that we must be exposing our children to something new and dangerous to their health.

   True   False   Cannot tell

                                 Answer

60. A plausible explanation of the increase could be that the principal age at which the condition is diagnosed has become lower.

   True   False   Cannot tell

                                 Answer

Passage 21

In Italy, there are about 17 mosquito species and six genera. Mosquitoes there are associated with every type of water body and include species with narrow and broad environmental requirements. They can be grouped according to oviposition site (water or land), overwintering stage (egg, larva or female), preferred host (mammals, birds or amphibians) and number of generations per year (one or many).

61. Would the following fact weaken the case made in the passage: no species of mosquito is found in brackish water?

   True   False   Cannot tell

                                 Answer

62. 'Genera' is a plural word meaning 'a class of things'.

   True   False   Cannot tell

                                 Answer

63. It can it be concluded from the information provided that all the species of mosquito need both aquatic and terrestrial environments during their life cycle.

True   False   Cannot tell

Answer [   ]

Passage 22

An atlas that is attributed to Christopher Saxton and printed around 1580 includes the earliest known printed plan of a city in the modern-day United States. Christopher Saxton was born an Englishman, in fact a Yorkshire man. His atlas contains five coloured charts created by the cartographer Giovanni Battista. They illustrate a survey of England and Wales, and the expedition of Sir Frances Drake to the West Indies and what is now the United States. For many generations the atlas formed part of the library of Sherburne Castle in Oxfordshire.

64. The volume contains the first printed map of England and Wales.

True   False   Cannot tell

Answer [   ]

65. By stating that the atlas is attributed to Christopher Saxton, the author is hinting that it may in fact not be his work.

True   False   Cannot tell

Answer [   ]

66. You can infer from the passage that the atlas was multifunctional.

    True   False   Cannot tell

                               Answer [   ]

Passage 23

Alcohol and tobacco are more harmful than illegal drugs such as cannabis and ecstasy, according to a new system that ranks drugs according to the estimated harm they cause. The system rates alcohol as only slightly less harmful than drugs such as heroin and cocaine. Tobacco appears in tenth place in the league table of 20 substances, well above the ranking of many illegal substances. Social harm, including crime, the cost to the state, and illnesses associated with a substance's use and whether or not it could be taken intravenously were considered in deciding the ranking. Alcohol and tobacco are responsible for 90 per cent of drug-related deaths in countries in which their use is legal.

67. You can infer from the passage that alcohol and tobacco's rating reflects their prevalence.

    True   False   Cannot tell

                               Answer [   ]

68. The main point made in the passage is that some legal drugs cause more harm than illegal ones.

    True   False   Cannot tell

                               Answer [   ]

69. Under the new system, cannabis is ranked in the lower half of the table of substances.

True   False   Cannot tell

Answer [   ]

Passage 24

Opponents complained that the decision was designed to socially engineer by discriminating against middle-class students. The chair of the Leader Teachers' Association had grave concerns over the change. Mr Langham said that it would encourage children to lie about their origins, and asked who is going to establish the veracity of the disclosures. Landowners could describe themselves as farmers, wealthy people who retire early could describe themselves as unemployed. The university admissions service has announced that information on the occupation, education and ethnicity of the parents of applicants will be made available to admissions officers. In the past this information was held back until after places were offered.

70. For the first time admissions officers will know if the parents of people applying to their university also went to university.

True   False   Cannot tell

Answer [   ]

71. You can infer from the passage that only middle-class applicants will be required to disclose this information.

True   False   Cannot tell

Answer [   ]

72. A synonym of 'veracity' is 'misconduct'.

    True   False   Cannot tell

                                     Answer   [   ]

Passage 25

Under section 36 of the Trade Descriptions Act 1968, goods are deemed to have been manufactured or produced in the country in which they last underwent a treatment or process resulting in a substantial change. Meat from animals coming into the UK and then cured here can be described as UK produce. Most well-known brands of ham or bacon are often advertised with packaging depicting a British countryside scene and described as 'farmhouse', which would lead shoppers to believe they are buying products made from British meat, but most are in fact made using imported meat.

73. The author of the passage believes that the practice risks some consumers being duped.

    True   False   Cannot tell

                                     Answer   [   ]

74. Under section 36 of the Act, British lamb exported to France and slaughtered there is sold as French.

    True   False   Cannot tell

                                     Answer   [   ]

75. The passage leads the reader to agree that the practice of importing foods and then processing them so that they are substantially changed should be stopped.

    True   False   Cannot tell

                                 Answer

Passage 26

If you choose to go to the theatre, stay in a hotel or catch a plane at one of the more popular times, it is usual for you to be charged the highest price. An influential report recently suggested that this principle should be extended to other activities, including essentials such as transport. If its recommendations were to be implemented, it would mean that we would be charged even higher fares on, for example, trains during the rush hour. It would also mean that we would be charged more to drive our cars at peak times. The level of charge suggested would have the effect of forcing many drivers off the road at these times.

76. At peak times drivers could avoid paying the highest band of charge by switching to public transport.

    True   False   Cannot tell

                                 Answer

77. You can infer from the passage that, to work, the proposal would require a charge for both the number of miles travelled and the time of the journey.

    True   False   Cannot tell

                                 Answer

78. The comparison made in the passage between the theatre and travel is flawed, because travellers who could not switch their journey to off-peak times would have no alternative but to pay more. You can choose to go to the theatre or stay in a hotel on a particular day, and if funds are short then you can take up the offer of a lower tariff at less popular times, or give up on the treat altogether. This flaw means that the proposed charges will fail to reduce congestion at peak times.

True   False   Cannot tell

                              Answer

Passage 27

What determines whether a product will succeed or fail? In 1990, six out of ten new products lasted for less than three months in the marketplace. In 2007, two out of ten succeeded. These products are all promoted and great emphasis is placed on brand and logo. Still, most fail and manufacturers must go a bit further if they are to improve the prospects of their product's success. Your iPod (you almost certainly have one) does not have a logo on it but it is instantly recognizable from its shape and feel. What about your mobile phone? There is a good chance it is a Nokia, and when it rings you immediately recognize the tone, which is a part of the Nokia brand. An incredible 60 per cent of people recognize it.

79. Given that the world's population is around 8 billion people, the passage suggests that approaching 5 billion people will recognize the Nokia ring tone.

True   False   Cannot tell

                              Answer

80. The author's strategy is to look at success stories.

    True   False   Cannot tell

                                   Answer

81. The passage is making the point that product success depends on more than a catchy brand name and a memorable logo.

    True   False   Cannot tell

                                   Answer

Passage 28

An old adage in economics was that 'When the United States sneezes the rest of the world catches a cold.' In the first half of 2007, growth in the United States slowed, while over the same period growth in the Eurozone accelerated and growth in Japan almost doubled. It still is true that the Central Southern American and Canadian economies remain susceptible to the importation of recession from the United States. But the spillover of a US recession to the rest of the world seems less likely these days because the US economy no longer has the same clout as it used to have.

82. The author would not agree that the US economy accounts for roughly the same proportion of global activity as it did 30 years ago.

    True   False   Cannot tell

                                   Answer

83. It seems we can conclude from the passage that we no longer have to look across the Atlantic or Pacific and panic every time the US cyclical activity takes a turn for the worse.

    True   False   Cannot tell

                                 Answer

84. The fact that the 2001 US recession was accompanied by a sharp slowdown in the rest of the world, while the 1982 US recession was not widely reflected, can be taken to be evidence in support of the hypotheses offered in the passage.

    True   False   Cannot tell

                                 Answer

Passage 29

March is a transitional month and can bring snow or warm weather. Last week saw balmy weather that ended with a bitter snap. No lasting damage was done and the trees and bushes that had shown the first sign of green and blossom bounced back. Spring flowers had appeared, and daffodils, hyacinths and primroses were an incredible sight in gardens and parks. The freeze put the burst of spring flowers on temporary hold.

85. The freeze lasted the whole of last week.

    True   False   Cannot tell

                                 Answer

86. You can't tell if it snowed this March, but from the passage you can infer that it would be unusual if it did.

   True   False   Cannot tell

                                 Answer

87. The warm weather triggered an early burst of spring flowers.

   True   False   Cannot tell

                                 Answer

Passage 30

The problem is not so great with hydroelectric schemes in temperate regions. But, before more hydropower schemes are built in tropical zones, the United Nations wants experts to examine the emissions produced by existing schemes and to recommend ways in which they can be made more environmentally friendly. A lot of the tropical hydropower plants were created by flooding forests, and as drowned plants and trees rot millions of tons of greenhouse gases are released. Despite burning no fossil fuels, the greenhouse emissions from these hydropower plants are higher than comparable fossil fuel-burning power plants. The most polluting hydropower installations are those that were created by the flooding of vast areas of carbon-rich land. These are usually shallow reservoirs, and over the first 10 years of their life it is estimated that they generate four times more greenhouse gases than equivalent modern coal-burning power stations to produce the same power output.

88.   The problem is not so great from hydroelectric schemes in temperate regions because the cooler temperatures mean that much less greenhouse gases are produced.

   True   False   Cannot tell

                              Answer

89.   You can infer that the United Nations does not think that using the movement of flowing water to drive turbines to generate electricity is necessarily a green source, even though it does not burn fossil fuels.

   True   False   Cannot tell

                              Answer

90.   The greenhouse gas that is largely responsible for the problem is methane, produced as the lush vegetation flooded by tropical reservoirs rots.

   True   False   Cannot tell

                              Answer

Passage 31

Even when policies seem gender-neutral they can still affect men and women differently. Soon laws will mean that all public bodies in every area, from health and education to transport, will have a new responsibility to demonstrate that they are treating men and women equally. The law is outcome-focused rather than process-driven. The test of fairness will be the measurement of the experience of men and women and the amount of progress towards stated improvements. The new duty will ensure that men and women are treated and targeted equally.

91. The new law might mean that a supermarket must change the way it advertises so that men or women respond equally to promotions.

     True   False   Cannot tell

                                  Answer   [   ]

92. It can be inferred from the passage that seemingly gender-neutral policies may affect men and women differently because men and women often have different needs.

     True   False   Cannot tell

                                  Answer   [   ]

93. The main idea of the passage is that the new law should be outcome-focused.

     True   False   Cannot tell

                                  Answer   [   ]

Passage 32

A massive increase in the amount of spam occurred last year, and spammers have moved from trying to sell fake medicines and counterfeit goods to what are called 'pump and dump' shares. It seems incredible, but spam-filtering companies report that the increase led to the amount of spam doubling, to the point where 19 out of 20 e-mails were unsolicited. This is not a claim to dismiss easily as an exaggeration, as it comes from the company responsible for filtering a quarter of all the world's e-mail traffic. The pump and dump shares are what are called 'penny shares' that the spammers promote through 100 million e-mails (a quarter of all spam), claiming that the price is about to increase rapidly. They only achieve a very low hit rate, but because they send out so many e-mails, enough people buy the shares that the price does rocket and the spammer is able to sell at a massive profit.

94. The intention of the author is to warn the reader that the very large rise in spam is coming from tricksters.

   True   False   Cannot tell

                                 Answer

95. A subordinate claim in the passage is that all unsolicited e-mail traffic is spam.

   True   False   Cannot tell

                                 Answer

96. The author finds it hard to believe that the problem got so bad that only 5 per cent of e-mails were solicited.

   True   False   Cannot tell

                                 Answer

Passage 33

A study that followed the health of 420,000 people who had used a mobile phone for an average of eight and a half years, in an effort to investigate the common fear of a link between their use and cancer, has published its findings. Some of the group had used a mobile since they were first introduced 20 years ago, and fears of a link have persisted throughout that period. If such a risk did exist, even a small one, then given the very widespread use of mobile phones it could cause thousands of additional tumours.

Anecdotal evidence and smaller earlier studies had suggested a higher rate of brain and neck cancer among phone users. The very large number of subjects in this study and the long period over which it was conducted mean we can have great confidence in the result. The study expected 15,000 tumours to occur in the sample population for the period, and a figure higher than this would suggest a link between the use of mobile phones and the risk of cancer.

97. The study found a small link between the use of mobile phones and the risk of cancer.

   True   False   Cannot tell

                                 Answer

98. You can correctly infer from the passage that the study involving 420,000 subjects is the most authoritative review yet of a link between cancer and the use of mobile phones.

   True   False   Cannot tell

                                 Answer

99. After 20 years, scientists should at last be able to state with confidence whether or not mobile phones cause cancer.

   True   False   Cannot tell

                                 Answer

100. If true, the fact that more than 15,000 tumours occurred in the sample would weaken the conclusion of the passage.

   True   False   Cannot tell

                                 Answer

Written assessments, presentations, group exercises and assessment centres

If you are invited to an assessment centre, the best approach is to set out to enjoy the day! They should do absolutely everything they can to make you feel at ease, and you can look forward to the chance to meet other candidates. Yes, it will be mentally challenging and tiring, but attend determined to give it your best shot and that way you will maximize your chances of coming out of the day with a job offer.

Written assessments, presentations, group exercises – all these test, among a number of things, your verbal reasoning skills, both written and spoken. You will most often face them at an assessment centre. You are invited to attend with a group of other applicants and will spend many hours in the company of representatives of the prospective employer and recruitment professionals, and you will be subjected to a range of assignments and interviews. It is not uncommon for the event to be held at a hotel and in some instances you may be invited to arrive the night before and be provided with overnight accommodation.

For obvious reason of cost, these events feature late in the recruitment process when the vast majority of candidates have been eliminated. If you are invited to one, congratulate yourself for getting through to this late stage. Many other applicants will have been disappointed. You can take it that the employer is very interested in you and is prepared to invest a considerable sum of money in taking a long, careful look at your potential. They will seek to use the event to form as objective an assessment of you as they can. In their eyes you will no longer be another application form or test paper result, but an individual they want to meet and get to know. They will also want you to be interested in them and to have thought carefully about why you want to join their organization. To answer this question properly you will need to have undertaken a careful look at the company, its services or products, and sector or sectors of operation. Unfortunately it is no longer sufficient to tell a prospective employer that you have had a look at its website. Attend armed with the benefits of a careful look at the organization overall, the section in which you would like to be placed and the position for which you have applied.

The time you spend and what you do at an assessment centre will vary from centre to centre and between recruitment campaigns. The experience may also vary slightly between candidates because some will, for example, undertake the interview first, followed by a written exercise, while others will undertake the written assignment first and then the interview. Things are organized in this way to manage resources efficiently and to reduce the time you spend hanging around waiting your turn. Organizations will inform you of an outline of what your day at the centre will comprise. You can glean a lot of very useful information from what you are sent, especially any information about the competencies examined. Read between the lines and you will be able to decide on the approach you will take.

An example of what such a day might include

The most important thing to take with you when you attend the centre is suitable ID. For reasons of test security, administrators will want to be able to confirm that no one is impersonating you and attending on your behalf. Read carefully and follow the instructions on your invitation and contact the organizers if you have any questions. They will provide you with everything you need or are allowed in terms of pens, scrap paper, calculators and so on. It would be a big mistake to arrive late for your appointment, so locate the centre and make sure you can find it with time to spare.

Many assessment events are organized with a number of common components. These include:

- Group exercises. These are sometimes called role-play exercises. In a group of usually five people you discuss a series of subjects. Before joining the group you are given a topic and briefing notes, and are allowed time to prepare. In the exercise you take turns introducing topics and have to discuss consensually. Assessors observe.
- Presentations. You're given a brief and time to prepare your topic. You then present this topic to an assessor, followed by questions. There are likely to be observers making notes.
- Written exercises. You're given a booklet of documents from different sources (press reports, semi-technical documents, etc) sometimes amounting to a lot of material. You read all the background information and assess it against a number of given criteria. You write up your findings, make recommendations and evaluate your decisions. The exercise is most likely to be completed on a PC.
- Interviews. The day is bound to include one or more panel interviews. You will face a panel of up to three people; one will lead. If you are applying for a professional or technical role you may face a technical interview as well.

These assessments will be competency-based. This means that the assignment will be used to test a given list of behaviour traits that are taken to be indicative of a desired quality. These might include any number of features such as communication skills, drive, decision making, relationship building, team work and so on. The relationships between the various assignments and the competencies are likely to be set out on a matrix like the graph shown here.

No.	Competency tested:	Determination	Development of ideas	Decision making	Planning	Team work	Written communication
1	Group exercise	*	*		*	*	*
2	Written exercise			*	*		*
3	Presentation		*	*			
4	Interview	*				*	

This graph shows the link between an assessment and the competencies it is used to investigate. In practice, more competencies would be investigated than shown here. It is common for candidates to be told the competencies that will be investigated and, as already mentioned, this information can be used to plan your approach to the assessments.

Below I consider in more detail and offer insights and tips on how best to approach group exercises, presentations, written exercises and self-assessment exercises. A mock assessment centre can be found at www.gradjobs.co.uk.

The group exercise or role-play

The topic or topics you are assigned to discuss vary from company to company, but you will find that group exercises are fundamentally similar in that you will be one of number of candidates and you must engage in consensual discussion.

1. Preparation time

Group exercises start with time to prepare. During the preparation time, list points that you feel are very important and make sure that these come up in the discussion. Don't worry if someone raises one of your points before you got the chance to make it; just contribute to its discussion and help develop the issue.

Sometimes you will get to meet the other candidates before the exercise starts; if you do, use this time to get to know them. You most likely will be told not to appoint a chairperson. Aim to play to your strengths. If maths is your thing, use the data they give you to work out some relevant figures (you should include figures even if maths is not you thing). It is vital to listen to others. They will be looking to see if your input helps to move the group forward, and whether you help the group to achieve its objectives.

In some cases you are given a great deal of briefing information – almost more than you can read in the time allowed. If this is the case, review the material quickly and keep your notes very brief. You might decide on an assessment tool to help in the handling of the briefing papers; examples include SWOT and PEST (strengths, weaknesses, opportunities, threats; and political, social, economic, technological). Another commonly used tool is the spider diagram, which is great for speed, recall and the emphasis of connections. Prepare these tools and think through these strategies before the day.

If you find that you do not have enough time to read all the background material, then decide what you want to say and use the time you have to make absolutely sure you have sufficient evidence to back up what you plan to say. Don't forget to include figures.

You are likely to be briefed as a group, and these are the people with whom you will discuss the topics. If it is appropriate and the opportunity presents itself, take the trouble to get to know some of the group. This will really help with any nervousness you may suffer. You will find it so much easier to have a constructive conversation with someone you have talked to before.

2. The discussion

The discussion will be observed and notes taken by the assessors; it may even be recorded on video. Push all this out of your mind as much as possible and keep your thoughts on the group, its objective and the discussion.

Try to avoid taking notes during the exercise. If you really must take notes, keep them extremely brief – just one-word notes – as you really do not want the invigilator to notice that you are 'looking down'. You want them to notice lots of eye contact and nods in agreement and to conclude that you can listen and have understood the significance of the contribution of others by modifying your position to take account of their contribution.

If you can, and the opportunity presents itself, speak first so that you make the first impression and demonstrate drive. Don't worry if your position is entirely different from everyone else's; you are being assessed on how you make your case, not what case you are making. So set out to make as good a case as you can for the view that you are representing, but also point out its weaknesses. Make sure you are enthusiastic even when discussing what might seem very mundane issues.

Be assertive in getting your points across, but be very careful not to stray into language that could be taken as aggressive. Listen as well as talk. Do make lots of eye contact and do nod in agreement, but don't shake you head or demonstrate your disagreement through body language. Consider making explicit reference to how you have modified your case to take into account the contributions of others. Do this by, for example, offering supportive summaries of others' contributions and then adding a further relevant point of your own.

Recognize the talents and merit in other people's contribution without diminishing your own. Use 'us' and 'we' to emphasize the collective purpose. Suggest criteria to clarify and evaluate the project. Help draw out quieter candidates by creating the space for them to speak. Do this by helping to ensure that everyone has a say. Show decisiveness and leadership qualities but avoid adopting the role of chair.

Don't take criticism personally. Don't start or get sucked into an argument, but in the unlikely event that one occurs, try to help make peace between the parties. This is important and a point on which many otherwise good candidates fail, so be sure to show empathy and go out of your way to resolve tension or disputes that arise between the other parties.

Be prepared to adopt the suggestions of others over your own, as this will be taken as an indication of your willingness to support another's project, of flexibility and of a talent in the building of relationships. Be constructive in your contributions and be supportive of others in your group. Keep your contributions to the point and spell out the relevance if you refer to something not immediately significant to the issue under discussion. Remember to back up all your points with facts and figures from the background material.

3. Self-evaluation of your performance

It is common for you to be asked to complete a self-assessment of your performance at an assessment centre. Take this exercise seriously as it is often scored and counts towards your overall mark. If appropriate, comment on both what you learnt from it and on how you might improve, were you to attend the event or take the exercise again. Keep your self-criticism positive but be sure it is genuine. You might comment on, for example, how productive your relationship building was, the impact of your communication, or how the group could have better developed the assignment.

Many candidates find critical self-evaluation a challenge; we are all so used to hiding our weaknesses and promoting our strengths. But realize that otherwise very strong candidates fail because they have not been open enough about their weaknesses and have not taken the opportunity to describe the strategies they have devised to address them.

Presentations

There is a lot you can do before the day to prepare for your presentation.

1. Plan something to say on core issues relevant to most subjects

Every sector of industry has issues that are relevant to pretty well every scenario. They depend on the industry of course, but might include recent legislation, the environment, health and safety, equality of opportunity, inclusiveness of people with disabilities (don't only think wheelchairs but include all types of disability) and social inclusion generally. There are bound to be cross-cutting themes relevant to the organization to which you have applied, so research them. The opportunity may arise where you can refer to these issues and gain valuable points.

2. Decide in advance how you might structure your presentation

You are unlikely to know the subject of your presentation until a short time before you have to make it, but this does not mean that you cannot do some preparation on the possible structure you intend to use. In the introduction you may want to summarize what you intend to go on to say and then in your conclusion review what you have said. There are some very good publications on the making of successful presentations; they may be worth a look.

You might decide to start by stating succinctly the assignment and go on to describe why addressing the issue is useful or necessary. If appropriate you could then review the file material (people, budget, rules) or background. Headings after that point might include Actions, Recommendations, Alternatives, Conclusion. Do not forget that it is essential that you show enthusiasm throughout.

3. Practise getting your timing right

You may not yet know how long you will have to present, but all the same it is worth practising how much you can say effectively in the usual time slots allocated in these exercises. On the day you will be allocated something between 10 and 20 minutes and you do not want to finish short or overrun. To get it right you need to have some experience of how long it will take to present a series of points with impact. Try to say too much or too little and you may end up disappointed with your presentation. Listen to a few public speakers on the radio, for example, and study how they make a point with impact and how long it takes them. You do not want to find yourself unable to cover all the points you planned to make and to be told to stop before you have made your concluding remarks.

4. The briefing and preparation time

You are often given a number of subjects from which to choose and are always provided with a briefing pack on the subject and told the time you have to prepare your presentation. Don't make the mistake of thinking you have to comment on all the subjects, including the ones you did not select. So, at the briefing, get absolutely clear in your mind the nature of the assignment and if in doubt ask someone for clarification. Be warned that it is common for the amount of time allowed for studying the back-ground papers to be very tight. These events are sometimes orga-nized so that the time allowed for reading the papers and preparing your presentation are combined, so be very careful not to spend too much time reading the papers and finding yourself with insufficient time to prepare your presentation.

Be sure to present the difficulties as well as the advantages of your approach to the topic. Often you are asked to provide some-thing original on the subject. Even if you are not specifically asked to do this, is may be worth offering a novel aspect to you presentation and then go on to examine the benefits and challenges to this aspect (don't forget to identify it as an original contribution). The relevance of everything you say should be clear or be explained. In practice, the invigilators don't so much care what you decide on but judge you on how you explain, justify and criticize it.

Once you have decided what to say, settle on your structure and make clear legible notes to which you can refer when making the presentation, and resolve to keep to it. Allocate an amount of time to each part of your presentation. Do not try to write out verbatim what you hope to cover. Even if you could manage it in the time allowed, the exercise is not one of you having to read your essay out loud. Instead, try numbering your points and commit these numbers and key words belonging to the points to memory. Try labelling them with one-word reminders and memorizing these. Try anything that works for you and will help you recall the points you want to make without excessive reference to your notes.

Remember to work quickly, as you may find you have very little time to prepare for your presentation.

5. Your presentation

Nerves aside, your presentation is likely to be as good or bad as your preparation, both before the day and during the preparation time. They are not expecting a polished public performance, but do be sure to speak clearly, make eye contact and try to keep reference to your notes to a minimum. Do think on your feet and adapt what you say as you speak, then revert back to your structure. Keep an eye on the time and try as much as possible to keep to the limits you set to speaking on each part of your presentation. If you find yourself going over time, drop some points. As already said, it is more important to deliver a timely presentation than be asked to stop before you have reached your conclusions. You are very likely to get the opportunity to raise further points and add details in the question and answer session that follows.

6. Follow-up questions/discussion

In these exercises it is common for more time to be spent answering questions and discussing what you said with the invigilator than you spent making your presentation.

It will help if you think of this time more as a brainstorming session than a cross-examination. So approach it with an open, curious mind rather than risk being perceived as defensive. During questions, the invigilator may follow up your response and keep asking follow-up questions until they feel they have the measure of you. At some point they will have decided whether you have made the grade, but they may still keep asking questions until you run out of things to say. Don't let this undermine your self-confidence and don't take offence. When the next line of questioning begins, it's a fresh start, a new line of enquiry, and you should have a different line of responses. Avoid falling back to a previous response, ie avoid repeating yourself. At all times make sure your response is relevant to the question and the line of enquiry. Listening skills are as important here as they are in the group exercise. Expect there to be one person who leads the questions and one or more others who mainly observe and take notes.

7. Self-assessment

If you are required to complete a self-assessment of your performance in the presentation exercise then take it seriously and complete it to the best of you ability; a score of what you write may feature as apart of your overall assessment. See the note on self-assessment, above.

Written exercises

1. Overview

These are tests of your ability to handle information, organize it and communicate in writing. You will be presented with a file of papers that provide information on a subject. It may include conflicting information that you have to evaluate and make recommendations about. Your task is to analyse the papers and prepare a note that builds a balanced and convincing case. To do this you will need to compare and contrast the options, using the stated criteria or proposing your own, and explain convincingly the reasons for your recommendation. These exercises are nearly always completed on a computer, so make sure your keyboard skills are up to scratch.

2. Planning in advance

Again, you can undertake some useful preparation before the day. One thing to consider is the style of approach that you adopt. This decision will depend in part on your background and your strengths; it is obvious that you should play to these. It should also be dependent on the role for which you are applying. By this I mean, if you are applying for a role in business then adopt a business style of report writing, with an executive summary stating the recommendation and summarizing the whole document, the main body and then the conclusion. If you are applying to an academic institution then a university style of report may be more appropriate and, if you can, adopt an elegant, fluid, readable written style. Research on the internet the style of reports and publications used in the organization or industrial sector in which they operate and, if you are confident to do so, adopt this style in the written exercise. That way you will appear well suited to the position. If producing a written document is really not your thing, consider using (but not excessively) bullet points and underlined headings to help convey you message. Illustrate points, where applicable: they will be far more convincing. If you find that you have not included numbers in your note, then you have probably not done as well as you could, so where practical back up and provide numerical evidence for what you say. Many organizations are looking for you to provide evidence of the case or point you make, so refer to figures or passages in the background paper and remember to source references.

Before the day it may be useful to give thought to analytical tools or processes to which you might refer or use in the exercise. Some have already been mentioned, including SWOT and PEST (see above). Consider if there are any core issues to which you might make reference in your paper that are applicable to most issues in the industrial sector to which you are applying. Look at reports and studies on the internet to identify possible issues. They might include, for example, equality of opportunity, reaching the hard to reach or challenging members of our society, or the contributions and/or threats technological advances might bring.

A common question asked is, how much should I write? The answer is that, within reason, what matters is not how much you write but what you write. Some assignments stipulate the extent expected, others do not. When no extent is indicated, set out to write enough to get the job done well. Don't write without good purpose, and take care to use the correct grammar, spelling and punctuation. Write too much and you increase the risk of errors and have less time to find any errors you may have made.

3. The briefing and preparation time

When you come to take the assignment it is very likely that you will be briefed on the exercise and provided with background or briefing papers. You may have a lot of information to go through and the time allowed to complete this part of the task may be tight. Be sure not to get caught out by the time limit. Get clear the aim of the exercise as explained to you and, first and foremost, use the time allowed to obtain the information necessary to serve the objective of the assignment. Then set about deciding the line to take in your paper and the structure that you will adopt.

4. The written assignment itself

Much of what you have done during your education and working career to date will serve you well in a written exercise. Take confidence from the fact that you have the skill to succeed in this assessment and apply what you have prepared before the day and during the briefing and preparation time. Although the written assignment is almost certainly to be administered on a PC, think back to the written exams at school or university for an idea of what to expect and insight into the best approach. Start with a note of the structure that you have decided to adopt and then use your time to implement that plan. Take care over grammar and spelling. Remember the invigilators are looking to see how well you can structure an argument and examine a number of options, recommending one. Where appropriate, use illustrations to make your points; back up what you say with figures; consider rather than quote from the background information, paraphrasing it or restating the passage in your own words. Demonstrate your ability at handling numerical information by offering clear, succinct restatements of relevant data in the background information. Remember to reference sources. Be convincing while remaining impartial and objective.

Five timed realistic tests with interpretations of your score

This chapter provides five practice tests made up of over 200 questions designed so that you may develop a good exam technique and improve your stamina and endurance under test conditions.

In each test the time allowed, number and level of difficulty of the questions, and the competencies tested are similar to real tests used by employers. Undertake these tests under conditions as realistic as possible by finding yourself a quiet place where you will be able to work for the suggested time limit without interruption. Approach each test as if it were the real thing and be sure that you apply the sheer hard work and continuous concentration essential for a good score in a real test. Practise the effective management of your time and remember not to spend too long on any one question.

To create a truly realistic test experience, set yourself the personal challenge of trying to beat your last score each time you take one of these practice tests. You will need to try really hard and take the challenge seriously if you are to realize this aim.

After each test review your answers and go over the explanations to any questions that you got wrong. You should aim to understand better the gaps in your knowledge, and before you take the next test, set about further practice of the sort found in earlier chapters with the intention of reviewing the principles you do not fully understand. Use the interpretation of your score to determine the amount and type of practice you still need.

Test 1. Synonyms and antonyms

In this test you must attempt 40 questions in 15 minutes. In each question you are presented with a pair of words and another word with list of suggested pairs. It is your task to identify the common link between the words. First work out if the given pair are synonyms or antonyms and then select the synonym or antonym of the second word from the list of suggested pairs. Record your answer A, B or C in the answer box.

Synonym or antonym means the word that is closest or most different in meaning. For example:

Sit is to stand as:
wander is to: A. meander   B. march   C. stroll

Answer

Answer: B

Explanation: sit and stand are antonyms as are wander and march, while meander and stroll are synonyms of wander. (Expect much harder questions than this in the test.)

Set a watch or stopwatch function on, for example, a mobile phone to the time allowed. Work where you will be free of distractions and 'really go for it' by trying to get the very best score you can.

Do not turn the page until you are ready to begin.

1. vocation is to career as:
   plebiscite is to: A. worker   B. referendum   C. decree

   Answer [   ]

2. lucid is to intelligible as:
   static is to: A. stationery   B. stationer   C. stationary

   Answer [   ]

3. malicious is to commendatory as:
   clamorous is to: A. raucous   B. muted   C. vociferous

   Answer [   ]

4. archaic is to dated as:
   integral is to: A. requisite   B. peripheral   C. fragmented

   Answer [   ]

5. veto is to interdict as:
   ratify is to: A. eschewal   B. endorse   C. repudiate

   Answer [   ]

6. momentous is to customary as:
   prosperous is to: A. distressed   B. burgeoning   C. serious

   Answer [   ]

7. emulate is to echo as:
   apostrophe is to: A. punctuation   B. technique   C. prayer

   Answer [   ]

8. naïve is to sophisticated as:
   sophisticate is to: A. avant-garde   B. provincial
   C. cosmopolitan

   Answer [   ]

9. autocratic is to enlightened as:
   relinquish is to: A. resist   B. bend   C. withhold

   Answer [   ]

10. come by is to procure as:
    adolescent is to: A. minority   B. juvenile   C. generation

    Answer [   ]

11. fluent is to inarticulate as:
    exhilarating is to: A. banal   B. lingering   C. invigorate

    Answer [   ]

12. amble is to hasten as:
    aligned is to: A. in order   B. affiliate   C. neutral

    Answer [   ]

13. parentheses is to enclosed information as:
    gerund is to: A. smoking   B. cigarette   C. health risk

    Answer [   ]

14. sanguine is to optimistic as:
    gloomy is to: A. bright   B. melancholy   C. respondent

    Answer [   ]

15. limited is to incalculable as:
    inimitable is to: A. homogeneous   B. distinctive
    C. idiosyncratic

    Answer [   ]

16. simile is to figure of speech as:
    figure of speech is to: A. diction   B. tragedy   C. paradox

    Answer [   ]

17. allegra is to glum as:
    irascible is to: A. surly   B. cordial   C. fractious

    Answer [   ]

18. allegory is to metaphor as:
    chasm is to: A. fissure   B. indent   C. fission

    Answer [   ]

19. brilliant is to inept as:
    remiss is to: A. negligent   B. attentive   C. cautious

    Answer [   ]

20. conqueror is to vanquisher as:
    caucus is to: A. notorious   B. numerous   C. nucleus

    Answer [   ]

21. fruitful is to futile as:
    inevitable is to: A. inexorable   B. ambivalent   C. assured

    Answer [   ]

22. compliant is to recalcitrant as:
    hub is to: A. middle   B. core   C. façade

    Answer [   ]

23. condescending is to contemptuous as:
    minuscule is to: A. diminutive   B. gargantuan
    C. prodigious

    Answer [   ]

24. prophecy is to forecast as:
    ricochet is to: A. vivacity   B. bounce   C. enthusiasm

    Answer [   ]

25. relegate is to promote as:
    augment is to: A. embellish   B. increase   C. understate

    Answer

26. idealistic is to pragmatic as:
    vertical is to: A. width   B. stature   C. measurement

    Answer

27. couple is to brace as:
    debacle is to: A. successor   B. triumph   C. farce

    Answer

28. unrelenting is to half-hearted as:
    automatic is to: A. conscious   B. robotic   C. instinctive

    Answer

29. privation is to want as:
    good humoured is to: A. amiable   B. peeved   C. irked

    Answer

30. dreary is to wretched as:
    singular is to: A. pleural   B. occasion   C. uncommon

    Answer

31. rebuke is to commend as:
    numerous is to: A. few   B. copious   C. integer

    Answer

32. noiselessly is to audibly as:
    postscript is to: A. appendix   B. epilogue   C. prologue

    Answer

33. lessen is to subside as:
    raw is to: A. prepared   B. naïve   C. strong

    Answer [   ]

34. accomplished is to incompetent as:
    inconsequential is to: A. inconsiderable   B. momentous
    C. peripheral

    Answer [   ]

35. supplicate is to appeal as:
    recess is to: A. gone   B. go   C. gap

    Answer [   ]

36. lethargy is to vigour as:
    somewhat is to: A. greatly   B. to a point   C. slightly

    Answer [   ]

37. exorbitant is to inflated as:
    roe is to: A. quarrel   B. ovum   C. dispute

    Answer [   ]

38. confident is to tremulous as:
    provide is to: A. refuse   B. bestow   C. substantiate

    Answer [   ]

39. animosity is to rancour as:
    straighten is to: A. truthful   B. distort   C. settle

    Answer [   ]

40. recommence is to suspend as:
    nonchalant is to: A. carefree   B. beleaguered   C. tirade

    Answer [   ]

End of test.

Test 2. Sentence sequence

You are allowed 25 minutes to complete this test, which comprises 40 questions. Each question comprises four sentences. The sentences are identified by the letters A to D, but the order in which they were originally written has been lost and most of the sentences are now in the wrong order. Your task is to put the sentences into the correct or original order.

Record your answer by placing the letters in the answer box in the order in which you think they were originally.

Set a watch or stopwatch function on, for example, a mobile phone to the time allowed. Work where you will be free of distractions and complete the test in one sitting.

Do not turn over the page until you are ready to begin.

1.

A. A professional homeopath, as a result of education, training and clinical experience, is competent to treat patients presenting with a wide variety of conditions. **B.** No one system can deal with all that an individual may need, or serve the entire population. **C.** Homeopathy may not always be the most appropriate form of treatment. **D.** Homeopathy is a unique system and therapeutic discipline that fulfils an important role in healthcare; it serves to prevent ill-health as well as being of benefit to most patients with both acute and chronic diseases.

Answer

2.

A. If, however, there is an opposing piece in the next black square, and an empty black square beyond it, then that piece may be captured and removed from the board by jumping over it. **B.** Black always has the first move. **C.** Sometimes several pieces can be taken like this in a single row and the winner is the player who either captures all his or her opponent's pieces or blocks them so that they cannot move. **D.** A move is made by advancing a piece diagonally forward into an empty black square touching the one it is currently in.

Answer

3.

A. In those days shields were very large, and rose at the middle into two peaks with a hollow between them, so that Thafta, seen far off in the sea, with its two chief mountain peaks and a cloven valley between them, looked exactly like a shield. **B.** Long ago in the small and mountainous island of Thafta lived a king named Umonico. **C.** The country was so rough that people kept no horses, but there were plenty of cattle. **D.** People used to say that Thafta 'lay like a shield upon the sea', which sounds as though it was a very flat country.

Answer

4.
A. Once you've sat down somewhere inconvenient, do not spring up just because you've been asked politely. **B.** The quickest way to do this is to park on a double yellow line, which is the daily street protest undertaken by most city dwellers. **C.** To start this, you need to park yourself somewhere where the police will have to move you on. **D.** Civil disobedience is a legal requirement of any demonstration.

Answer [   ]

5.
A. The range, manufactured by electronics giant Gizzmo, comprises an internet-enabled washing machine, microwave oven and air conditioning unit, as well as the first 'smart fridge', which has an internet connection and the capacity to form the hub of a future home network. **B.** The technology involved is already available to consumers. **C.** Home networking, as it's called, connects every appliance in the home, from your PC to your central heating, via a central hub, which can then be accessed and controlled via the internet. **D.** Indeed, one company has already launched the first range of such appliances in the UK.

Answer [   ]

6.
A. The Trojans gathered on a height in the plain, and Hector, shining in armour, went here and there, in front and rear, like a star that now gleams forth and now is hidden in a cloud. **B.** With dawn Agamemnon awoke, and fear had gone out of his heart. **C.** Then a great black cloud spread over the sky, and red was the rain that fell from it. **D.** He put on his armour, and arrayed the chiefs on foot in front of their chariots, and behind them came the spearmen, with the bowmen and slingers on the wings of the army.

Answer [   ]

7.
A. At 3,560 feet, Snowdon is the highest mountain south of the Scottish Highlands. B. Its 845 square miles make only a slightly smaller area than the 866 square miles of the English Lake District. C. Snowdonia is the second largest national park in Great Britain. D. Over 500,000 people climb it each year.

Answer [   ]

8.
A. They may seem like an arcane field of investigation: after all, are there not more pressing problems with extant species? B. But the development of a species, its transformations and final extinction are all elements that can be applied to current-day biology. C. Their closest living relative is the horseshoe crab. D. Trilobites roamed the world's oceans some 500 million years ago.

Answer [   ]

9.
A. The huge amount of energy is radiated out from the core and some eventually reaches Earth, keeping us alive. B. It has been doing this for 4,500 million years, but is still only halfway through its lifetime. C. The sun is using up its mass at the rate of 4 million tonnes each second! D. It is a middle-aged star.

Answer [   ]

10.
A. The same applies to spacecraft that operate in places where there is no atmosphere at all. B. Jet airliners fly at heights of 10,000 metres or more. C. Such aircraft are said to be pressurized. D. At such heights the atmosphere is so thin that the aircraft must have its own air supply with oxygen at the normal pressure.

Answer [   ]

11.
A. This is usually caused by a reaction to pollen, and is therefore particularly common when flowers are open. **B.** The eyes may be affected in the same way, becoming itchy, sore and weepy. **C.** Many people suffer from hay fever. **D.** The lining of the nasal cavity becomes sensitive and inflamed and produces a large amount of mucus, so the nose runs and the person sneezes a lot.

Answer [   ]

12.
A. Particular finger positions or gestures of the hand, common to their age and civilization, delivered a message that was instantly recognized by those who understood the symbolism. **B.** Since ancient times hands have been used in cave paintings, drawings, sculpture and fine art as symbols of communication. **C.** European religious paintings represented the Holy Trinity by the extended thumb, index and middle fingers of a hand. **D.** Ancient Egyptian and Semitic art, for example, depicted celestial power by a hand painted in the sky.

Answer [   ]

13.
A. Without food, small birds can quickly starve to death. **B.** Somehow they must maintain reserves at a level that allows them to avoid both starvation and predation. **C.** Too little fat and they may starve to death, while too much increases the energy required for flight, causing them to be slower, less agile and more at risk of predation. **D.** To survive a long, cold night or periods during the day without eating, birds need to put on fat reserves.

Answer [   ]

14.

A. The sapwood is less dense and therefore softer than the heartwood. B. The heartwood is extremely dense and hard and its only job is to support the tree. C. It is therefore much wetter than the heartwood. D. It provides support too, but it also carries water and mineral salts (sap) up the trunk.

Answer [   ]

15.

A. A series of islands or chains in the head or heart lines may point to an imbalance of the biochemistry due to mineral deficiencies. B. It follows that any impairment of the lines reveals that the constitution is somehow weakened. C. Clear, strong lines in the hand are thought to reflect robust health. D. A similar effect on the life line reveals poor vitality and a weakened constitution.

Answer [   ]

16.

A. Its plan to increase the amount of municipal waste we recycle to 33 per cent by 2015 has been described as 'depressingly unambitious' by a parliamentary committee, as most Western nations have already surpassed this level. B. In parts of Belgium, for example, 72 per cent of biodegradable waste is recycled or composted, compared with about 11 per cent in the UK. C. The government has been criticized for its laissez-faire attitude. D. While other countries are well on their way to meeting the EU levels by recycling and composting, the UK is lagging far behind.

Answer [   ]

17.

A. The attacks are often brought on by pollen or dust, or occasionally by some kind of food to which the person is allergic. B. This makes it difficult to breathe and the person wheezes. C. Asthma is serious. D. The muscles in the walls of the bronchioles contract, so the tubes get narrower.

Answer [   ]

18.
A. A 20-year study has found that taking 300–400 micrograms a day of this B-vitamin can cut your risk by 20 per cent. **B.** Folic acid, long recommended to women trying to conceive, could prevent strokes too. **C.** It helps break down homocysteine, an amino acid that occurs naturally in the body and has been linked to artery-wall damage. **D.** Folic acid is found in broccoli, tomatoes, kidney beans, liver, some citrus fruits and leafy green vegetables such as spinach, or is available in pill form.

Answer _____

19.
A. If enlargement of the EU goes ahead, it will increase by 10 member states by the beginning of 2004. **B.** When these countries attain membership, hundreds of thousands will want to move to the west in search of higher incomes and, in time, as citizens of the EU, they will be perfectly entitled to do so. **C.** Arguably the most important fact about immigration is that in the next two decades much of it will be lawful. **D.** Much of the small print remains to be agreed, but it is likely that the EU will increase by 30 per cent.

Answer _____

20.
A. Under the plan the group would sell its private equity division to its management, who would then manage the $2 billion of investments owned by the group. **B.** The decision has forced the group to consider selling its own private equity operation in order to avoid a conflict of interest. **C.** The move would see Axis surrender control of its equity investments in favour of funds managed externally. **D.** Axis is preparing to invest $650 million in Ava Investors, the Orlando-based private equity firm set up to manage the wealth of the billionaire Savini family.

Answer _____

21.

A. Latuga's banks have lent £100 million at an annual negative interest rate of 1 per cent. **B.** This means that instead of Latuga paying interest on the loan, the banks will pay Latuga £1 million a year in interest. **C.** Latuga, the world's biggest producer of tinned greens, turned the banking world on its head by taking out the first ever negative interest loan. **D.** The banks were happy to agree the loan because it has allowed them to acquire bonds and shares, which are forecast to grow by as much as 5 per cent a year.

Answer

22.

A. The arts in the UK must to an observer seem to be booming, with new galleries opening in the capital to great acclaim, thriving regional institutions, and ambitious plans to open a major centre of contemporary art in the North West. **B.** Add to this the fact that three years ago the Chancellor gave the arts a considerable financial boost, and the National Lottery Fund has provided millions of pounds of lottery money to pay for new venues or renovating existing ones. **C.** Yet the Arts Council expresses fears that even after such record spending, some arts institutions are struggling to survive and risk financial collapse. **D.** There is some evidence to support this surprising view if one compares the funding for museums and galleries per capita across Europe, for then one realizes that the UK continues to lag behind its neighbours in arts expenditure.

Answer

23.

A. But if the government does about the nation's diet and level of exercise what it has done about most health risks such as smoking and drinking alcohol, which is very little or nothing, then the level of obesity will continue to rise and the health of the nation will continue to fall. **B.** In the face of such likely government inaction, the only real alternative engines for change are education and litigation, but unlike smoking and drinking there is nothing intrinsically unhealthy about eating, so it is hard to imagine how recourse to the courts could force change on the nation's eating habits. **C.** That leaves education, and given that fast-food chains and sugar drink companies have a massive presence in almost every campus, state school and even hospital, it is hard to imagine how the cash-starved educational institutions can alone counter the junk food movement. **D.** If the government is willing to regulate to force disclosure of the content of what we eat, get junk food out of schools, make available more healthy alternatives, and install bike racks in public places to encourage more exercise, then the health of the nation will improve.

Answer

24.

A. Some economists have been expressing fears for a considerable length of time about an unsustainable boom that could turn into a bust. **B.** The admission comes in a report to the Home Affairs Committee setting out the implications of the continued rise, fuelled by low unemployment, low interest rates and a shortage of housing stock. **C.** In a startling reversal the government has acknowledged that house price inflation is a significant problem rather than just an issue. **D.** The report identified that the issue became a problem for first-time buyers in London and the South East, and for professionals who could not afford to live in this region, so creating shortages of essential workers in hospitals, schools and the Civil Service.

Answer

25.

A. This time a synchronized recession took place whereby all the major economies slowed down and took with them many others, including Argentina, Mexico, Singapore and Taiwan. **B.** The IT and telecommunications-driven fall in investment expenditure began in the United States and spread to the world's other economies, leading to worldwide economic recession. **C.** The bursting of the hi-tech bubble is the most important reason for the slowing growth, but it has been made worse by the fact that each of the major economies has its own home-grown problems, which exacerbated the downturn. **D.** In the two previous economic downturns, one or more of the biggest economies has been able to avoid recession.

Answer

26.

A. Fay travelled to the same destination by train third class, with her battered suitcase and few possessions; she hoped to find work teaching English but when the war intervened she volunteered to work in a Red Cross hospital. **B.** The two women were to meet in the great city under the most unlikely circumstances. **C.** Her family had fallen out of the middle class into poverty, and her marriage to a second-rate musician had ended sterile and pointless, but she looked forward to a new life with courage and enthusiasm. **D.** Lorenza went to Roma in a chauffeur-driven limousine; she was the daughter of a Venetian aristocrat whose family boasted two Doges from the 17th century, and her life to that point had been typical of her class, with high society parties and travel.

Answer

27.

A. First, our economy is driven by expenditure on luxury goods, and because they are luxury they are non-essential and so can be avoided altogether if the price becomes too great or the spare cash we have in our pocket each month becomes too little. **B.** Second, the potential housing bubble and the difficulty being experienced by public sector workers struggling to afford a home is peculiar to the South East, so why apply a general interest rate increase in an effort to address a regional problem? **C.** I would argue that interest rates should be left unchanged, and nothing be done to the rate in order to tackle a housing problem that is not creating general inflationary pressure. **D.** The property boom and the profits people are making from it may be the only thing preventing our economy sliding into recession, so why risk it?

Answer [   ]

28.

A. Hard on her heels is the US Deputy Secretary of State, who is expected to emphasize the fact that they also expect a crackdown on its most polluting industries as a matter of urgency in order to ensure that the entry conditions to the treaty are realized. **B.** In the diplomatic game of grandmother's footsteps, in which the world powers try to coax China to sign the environmental treaty, they seem to have forced the Beijing authorities to realize that they must take the first half step. **C.** If the authorities fail to control the level of emissions they are vulnerable to the unfair charge that corruption is preventing action; this, on top of the threatened diplomatic and economic isolation, is thought to be sufficient to ensure China will become both a signatory and a compliant member within the next three years. **D.** Today the President of the European Union will deliver to the Chinese authorities the uncompromising message, endorsed by the Union Member States, that failure to follow words with actions could lead to diplomatic isolation.

Answer [   ]

29.
A. The areas of the country identified with the worst problems were mainly located in the South East of the country, along with North Yorkshire and the Lake District. **B.** It comes on the day a senior minister called for 100,000 new homes a year to be built in villages and hamlets to create and sustain populations large enough to support rural shops and schools. **C.** The need for more and better homes was reported to be most acute in the social housing sector, yet that sector was dwindling as tenants exercised the right to buy in areas of high demand, where thousands of people on low incomes or living on benefits are priced out of the property market. **D.** The need for more social housing is outlined in a stark report from the Countryside Agency, the government's main adviser on rural issues, which was published today.

Answer

30.
A. The commission also wants insurers to be legally bound to provide compulsory cover for pedestrians and cyclists involved in accidents with cars. **B.** A shake up of the law governing the industry across Europe will make it far easier for individuals to switch insurance companies. **C.** Plans were announced by the European Commission that should lead to greater competition in the vehicle insurance market. **D.** It should mean that companies are no longer able to restrict the length of time motorists may keep their vehicles in EU states other than the ones in which they are registered.

Answer

31.

A. The Commission is drawing up a dossier of information to demonstrate to the Home Office that women are being unfairly excluded from the force and that the test has very little bearing on the work of the police. **B.** The Commission argues that a police officer very rarely has to run down the street after a criminal, and so whether or not they can run fast or have a firm grip is irrelevant to the job and prevents many able female applicants from becoming officers. **C.** The present test involves an endurance run and upper body and hand strength tests, which the Commission would like to see replaced with a health screening. **D.** The Equality Commission is pressing the Home Office to change the fitness test used for the recruitment of police officers, which it is argued is unfairly biased towards male applicants.

Answer

32.

A. The study found that 70 per cent of children reported that their dreams reflected their viewing habits, while only 60 per cent of adults reported that television influenced their dreams. **B.** Research has found that children's dreams are influenced more by television than adults', while adults' dreams are affected most by what they are reading. **C.** Fantasy books were linked to a higher rate of nightmares amongst both children and adults, with children, for example, reporting that scary books caused nightmares. **D.** The analysis found apparent links between respondents' dreams and the subject of their reading.

Answer

33.
A. Sunday's vote is expected to be noticeable in one other respect, as the socialist vote stood firm while generally the left vote collapsed. B. Sunday's vote places in perspective some of the more excitable commentary in the United States on France becoming a fascist state. C. On Sunday, when the second round of the French parliamentary elections is completed, it is likely that the country will have a president and parliament of the same political persuasion for the first time for a number of years. D. The far-right vote also collapsed because of the centre right's tougher policies on crime and immigration, and because of the poor standard of the right-wing candidates, many of whom hardly bothered to campaign.

Answer [   ]

34.
A. Epidemiologists know that the virus is by far the leading cause of human disease worldwide, infecting virtually all children before the age of 5. B. Fortunately, research has established much and the investigation has led to the trial of a vaccine, with promising results. C. Unlike bacteria that spread via contaminated water, meaning that people in the poorest parts of the world suffer disproportionately, the pathogen is found to be responsible for the same level of incident of disease in advanced nations such as the United States as in poor regions, including the Asian subcontinent. D. The virus's ubiquity is due to it being highly contagious and this means it is transmitted irrespective of sanitation.

Answer [   ]

35.
A. The proportion of over-50s using the internet to shop, chat, pursue hobbies and study has doubled. **B.** Eleven per cent of the over-50s population said that they have sold something over the internet, while one in four have bought something over the net in the past six months. **C.** However, a significant number of older people risk being left behind as the digital divide grows. **D.** Older people had been slow to adopt the technology but are now fast catching up; however, a significant minority remain offline despite the falling cost of the technology. Those on the lowest incomes and with the fewest qualifications are most likely to miss out on the digital revolution.

Answer ⬚

36.
A. The bullet-like silver digital radio is a great compact unit and is powered by two AA batteries, which provide around 20 hours of power, or through an in-car power jack point. **B.** The unit has a backlit LED screen and produces really good sound with great bass depth, the screen is easy to read and the unit can switch between mono and stereo mode. **C.** When travelling by car, reception quality is unfortunately intermittent especially when in built-up areas, so a regular but quick shift along the frequency bands is necessary to solve the problem. **D.** More expensive than other units, the quality and features put it ahead.

Answer ⬚

37.
A. The cells used would have to achieve the US Department of Energy's standard of 10 per cent water-splitting efficiency before the investment would be worthwhile and the output would approach the 10 litres level. B. If the rooftops of every house in the United States were covered in these cells, every household would have at its disposal the hydrogen equivalent of over 10 litres of petrol (gasoline) a day. C. There is much talk of a hydrogen economy, and one version of that future is described as based on dissociating water into hydrogen and oxygen, using sunlight in photo-catalyst cells or films. D. But this kind of efficiency has only been achieved under careful laboratory conditions using ultraviolet light. Sunlight comprises only 4 per cent ultraviolet light, so the search is still on for a photo-catalyst that reaches the same level of efficiency using the whole sunlight spectrum.

Answer [   ]

38.
A. I came to this proposition circuitously while studying chimpanzees and then orang-utans for over 17 years in their natural habitats. B. My proposition is not incompatible with the dominant view but it adds a role for a cultural input into the evolution of intelligence for all social species, whereas previous explanations saw a cultural input as uniquely human. C. A human child learns primarily from its parents and from the social and wider cultural context in which that family group lives; this also applies to the offspring of the great apes. D. The most influential explanation of intelligence is that it evolves in animals that live socially, as it allows them to form the most advantageous relationships and to react quickly to changes in social situations.

Answer [   ]

39.

A. The fourth assessment of global warming stated that it is unequivocal, will go on for centuries and very likely is man-made. B. The third assessment was produced in 2001 and stated that most of the warming over the past 50 years is likely to be due to the increase in greenhouse gas concentrations. C. In 1995 the third report concluded that the balance of evidence suggests a discernible human influence on global climate. D. And the first report in 1990, by comparison, asserted that warming is broadly consistent with current climate change models.

Answer

40.

A. The player must follow a fast-moving dance routine while standing on an interactive mat that feeds their movements back into the console. B. One hundred US children, all the offspring of public employees, received as a gift from their parents' health insurance provider, a free dance game and console. C. The insurance provider hopes that the results will be positive and as a consequence they will pay out fewer claims linked to the treatment of diseases triggered by obesity. D. The initiative is part of a study to see if such games can reduce the levels of obesity suffered by more than a third of public employees' children.

Answer

End of test.

Test 3. Word swap

This test comprises 40 questions. Allow yourself eight minutes to complete it.

Each question comprises a sentence in which two words have been swapped. What this means is that one word has been put in the place of another and that word has been put in the original word's place. No other words have been moved. Your task is to identify these two words and record them in the answer box. Be sure that you record the two words in the answer box as they appear in the sentence.

You will have to work very quickly if you are to attempt all 40 questions in the time allowed.

Set a watch or stopwatch function on, for example, a mobile phone to the time allowed. Work where you will be free of distractions and attempt the test in a single sitting.

Do not turn the page until you are ready to begin.

1. Though apparently a likable woman she sought acclaim, who could also be grand, a trait that tarnished her reputation.

   Answer [   ]

2. Boiling the substances ruins their cancer-fighting properties, while steaming, microwaving and stir-frying preserves the vegetables and are healthier cooking methods.

   Answer [   ]

3. The food and drink giant announced that aspartame, hydrogenated fats and monosodium glutamate would no longer be used in the manufacture of any of its food and soft drinks products.

   Answer [   ]

4. Consumer pressure has been largely responsible for supermarkets requiring suppliers to stop using the most harmful residues and making information available on pesticides in products.

   Answer [   ]

5. Stars account for only one component of the mass of the universe; the remainder is an invisible per cent called 'dark matter' that neither emits nor reflects light.

   Answer [   ]

6. The Taj Mahal took a team of 20,000 masons 17 years to build as a monument to Queen Mumtaz, Shah Jehan's wife and was beautiful to be as intended as she was beautiful.

   Answer [   ]

7. According to the Office for National Statistics, Poles were arriving to live in Britain at a rate of 1,500 a day and included immigrants, Zimbabweans, South Africans and Russians.

Answer

8. The Sorrentina Peninsula with its bay of lemon groves, multi-coloured buildings, backdrop of Mount Vesuvius and the acres of Naples has always had a seductive allure.

Answer

9. Rain and drizzle elsewhere become confined to southern England with a few brighter spells developing will.

Answer

10. The role is to implement and develop a clear sales plan for volume and margin growth by broadening the customer base and developing the market.

Answer

11. There is massive disparity in the living costs experienced by different types of households, with pensioners facing price rises of 7 per cent because of steep increases in energy bills, and middle-class families coping with a rate of over 8 per cent because of increases between university tuition fees.

Answer

12. We naturally have a sweet tooth and when has been one of the first things to be added it companies want to make a product a bit different.

Answer

13. Some 10 millennia ago people in the Middle East began to grow wheat, pulses and other cereals and lentils, and domesticated sheep, goats to eat and then for milk, cheese and wool.

Answer [   ]

14. After weeks of wet and often sunny weather the bank holiday weekend turned warm and windy.

Answer [   ]

15. Individuals who have a close family relative with bowel cancer normally raises the lifetime risk and two between four times.

Answer [   ]

16. Bats and birds fly in quite different ways, with bats generating thrust on only the up and down stroke while birds use both the down stroke.

Answer [   ]

17. Scientists discovered that indeed some people are more accident-prone than others when they confirmed that one in 29 people are 50 per cent more likely to suffer a mishap.

Answer [   ]

18. A study found that two in one 40-something employees want to quit their current job to earn less in a role that puts satisfaction before success.

Answer [   ]

19. The little ferry boat from Newtown Creek could not run this morning because the wind were too strong, an inconvenience and yet somewhat welcome reminder of how things was.

Answer

20. A conventional car that combines a petrol engine with an electric motor to reduce fuel consumption can achieve 65 miles per gallon and costs around £2,000 more than a similar hybrid vehicle.

Answer

21. The genetic sequence of a marsupial has been mapped and provided evolutionary insight into the important split between the two main branches of the mammal family tree.

Answer

22. The tea ceremony is a refinement of ritual, meditation and aesthetics and for 500 years has expressed the combination of Japanese culture.

Answer

23. Typically business is the lifeblood of every business and it comes down to getting paid for goods or services on time and avoiding delays to payments usually orchestrated by customers trying to finance their cashflow on the cheap.

Answer

24. The management candidate will be bright, numerate and enthusiastic and possess the skills of producing successful accounts, forecasts and draft accounts.

Answer

25. People who ate less salty food were found to have a 25 per cent lower risk of cardiac arrest or death and a 20 per cent lower risk of premature stroke.

Answer

26. Sales of British food and drinks abroad have reached a valuable £11 billion, helped by the return of beef exports to the rest of the EU, with whisky remaining the most record item.

Answer

27. Every day last year 200 children under the age of 11 were carrying home from school for sent out attacks on teachers and other children.

Answer

28. When Monet arrived in London to paint he would 'without the fog London said not be a beautiful city'.

Answer

29. The San Francisco disasters of 1906 were the worst natural earthquakes in US history.

Answer

30. One in five Britons leave abroad head for Australia, while large numbers moving for Spain, Canada and South Africa, which are also popular destinations.

Answer

31. Recent achievements have proved further stark evidence of the educational apartheid dividing the research of bright children from low and high income families.

    Answer [   ]

32. In some parts of the world and at some points in history, law is determined by the rule of the mob rather than the rule of justice.

    Answer [   ]

33. An environmental scientist who had previously held against nuclear power recently said that the building of new nuclear power stations is a necessary step if global warming is to be campaigned back.

    Answer [   ]

34. Widespread anger was voiced over the sheer waste of nurture and the cost to the economy of failing to talent so many of the nation's gifted children.

    Answer [   ]

35. You may be the victim of crime in a country that nationally enjoys a good judicial system, but if you where were the victim has an incompetent police force or prosecution service, then the result may be that justice is not done.

    Answer [   ]

36. The thought of our own mortality is something many people find comfortable and this, along with the fact that many people believe they have nothing to leave, is probably the reason who so few of us have not yet made a will.

    Answer [   ]

37. The vast majority of figures do not have a sufficient grasp of statistics to tell whether or not the citizens produced by their government are correct or being used correctly.

Answer

38. In defence of state schools, some commentators point out the important contribution their home life makes to achievement. They argue that a child needs parental encouragement and resources such as a quiet place to study if they are to realize that full potential.

Answer

39. The public also seemed more willing to reconsider nuclear power in a way that would have seemed impossible only a few years ago. Part of the reason for this change of heart is that they realize alternative renewable sources of power also bring unwelcome consequences.

Answer

40. Should we judge a 100 per cent conviction rate as inevitable sign of a successful or failing juridical system? It is surely a, desirable even, that some cases will be brought that fail at trial?

Answer

End of test.

Test 4. English usage

This test contains 40 questions and you are allowed 30 minutes in which to attempt them. Each test comprises four sentences labelled A to D. You are required to identify the suggested answer from a choice of four sentences that is most correct in terms of English usage. The solution may be a question of grammar, punctuation spelling or style.

Indicate your answer by writing the corresponding letter of the alphabet for the suggested answer of your choice in the answer box.

Work somewhere free of interruption and complete the test in one continuous period.

Do not turn the page until you are ready to begin.

1.
A. They were talking so aloud that I had trouble concentrating on my work.
B. They were talking so quietly that I had trouble concentrating on my work.
C. They were talking so loud that I had trouble concentrating on my work.
D. They were talking so loudly that I had trouble concentrating on my work.

Answer [   ]

2.
A. We were late because we stopped to visit the town we left two years ago.
B. We were late because of we stopped to visit the school we left six years ago.
C. We were late because we stopped to visit the city we left six years before.
D. We were late because of our stop to visit the church in which we were married three years before.

Answer [   ]

3. Which sentence includes an oxymoron?
A. On holiday we walked and swam a lot.
B. Sally corrected me by pointing out that she wanted tea instead of coffee.
C. The newspaper reported a growing anger towards the Government's policies.
D. He loved his aunt but found her kindness suffocating.

Answer [   ]

4.
A. It is not let to smoke in the doctor's surgery.
B. It is not permitted to smoke in the doctor's surgery.
C. Surprisingly, it is permit to smoke in the doctor's surgery.
D. It is not allowed to smoke in the doctor's surgery.

Answer [   ]

5.

A. The newspaper agreed to report that next Wednesday the couple had been married for 20 years.

B. The newspaper agreed to report that next Wednesday the couple will have been married for 20 years.

C. The newspaper agreed to report that next Wednesday the couple will be married for 20 years.

D. The newspaper agreed to report that next Wednesday the couple have been married for 20 years.

Answer

6.

A. The whole of all Venice was very almost under water.

B. All Venice was nearly practically under water.

C. The whole of Venice was pretty well almost under water.

D. All Venice was very nearly under water.

Answer

7.

A. You can see on the map that France is above Spain and below Germany.

B. You can see on the map that France is above Spain and under Germany.

C. You can see on the map that France is over Spain and under Germany.

D. You can see on the map that France is over Spain and below Germany.

Answer

8.

A. We don't have to work over the weekend to meet the deadline as we arrived to work on Monday morning to discover that the client announced an extension to the project.

B. We needn't have worked over the weekend to meet the deadline as this morning the client announced an extension to the project.

C. We didn't need to work over the weekend to meet the deadline as on Monday morning the client announced an extension to the project.

D. We mustn't work all weekend on the project as this morning the client announced an extension to the project.

Answer [   ]

9.

A. When or else fails this medicine is still effective.

B. When all else fails this medicine is still efficient.

C. When all other remedies fail this medicine is still efficient.

D. When all else fails this medicine is still effective.

Answer [   ]

10. Identify the statement in which the author uses irony:

A. His painting wasn't the best in the exhibition but it was certainly the biggest.

B. He was not feeling very hungry so he ordered an extra large main course and two deserts.

C. She was elected school representative and few would question her suitability for the role.

D. I was relieved when our team leader at work resigned, because she used to talk about people behind their back.

Answer [   ]

11.
A. He is so afraid that he would loose his way that he decided to walk till the town hall and then turn back.
B. He is so afraid that he would lose his way that he decided to walk to the town hall and then turn back.
C. He was so afraid that he would loose his way that he decided to walk till the town hall and then turn back.
D. He was so afraid that he would lose his way that he decided to walk to the town hall and then turn back.

Answer [   ]

12.
A. Only I and my sister went but the plane already left before we arrived.
B. Only my sister and I went but the plane already left before we arrived.
C. Only my sister and I went but the plane had already left before we arrived.
D. Only I and my sister went but the plane already left before we arrive.

Answer [   ]

13.
A. As usual they had to play football under the rain.
B. As usually they had to play football in the rain.
C. As usual they had to play football in the rain.
D. As usually they had to play football under the rain.

Answer [   ]

14.
A. It's better to save for the future rather than spend all your money today on treats and outings.
B. It's better to save for the future than to spend all your money today on treats and outings.
C. It's better to save for a rainy day rather than spend all your money today on treats and outings.
D. It's better to save for a rainy day to a certain extent than spend all you money on treats and outings.

Answer [   ]

15.

A. After the visit of his great aunt the tin of biscuits was nearly empty but at least a few were left.

B. After the visit of his great aunt the tin of biscuits was nearly empty but at least few were left.

C. After the visit of his great aunt the tin of biscuits was nearly empty but a least a little were left.

D. After the visit of his great aunt the tin of biscuits was nearly empty but a least little were left.

Answer

16.

A. The waitress refused taking the cigarettes even after the police showed to her the CCTV footage.

B. The waitress denied taking the cigarettes even after the police showed to her the CCTV footage.

C. The waitress refused taking the cigarettes even after the police showed the CCTV footage to her.

D. The waitress denied taking the cigarettes even after the police showed the CCTV footage to her.

Answer

17.

A. They said they would pay this week but no one really expected them to.

B. They believed they will pay this week but no one was really surprised when they didn't.

C. They say they would pay this week but no one really expected them to.

D. They said they will pay this week but no one was really surprised when they didn't.

Answer

18.

A. I apologize for my friend's offensiveness.

B. I apologizing for what I said to you.

C. I apologies for my friend's bad manners.

D. I insist you say sorry for my friend's rudeness.

Answer

19.
A. He sat in the shadow in the middle of the park and read his book out loud.
B. He sat in the shade in the centre of the park and played a game of cards.
C. He sat in the shade in the middle of the park and reflected on his situation.
D. He sat in the shadow in the centre of the park and worked out what he would say.

Answer [   ]

20.
A. It was only a Pug, which is a friendly breed of dog, but it was not afraid of nothing.
B. It was only a Boarder Terrier, which is a small breed of dog, but it was not afraid of nobody.
C. It was a Mastiff, which is a very large breed of dog, but it was afraid of anybody.
D. It was a Chihuahua, which is one of the smallest breeds of dog, but it was not afraid of anybody.

Answer [   ]

21.
A. Are you enjoy the play?
B. Are you enjoying the play?
C. Do you enjoy the play?
D. Do you enjoying the play?

Answer [   ]

22.
A. The cost of the item paid by the retailer is far less than the cost asked for it in the shop.
B. The cost of the item paid by the retailer is far less than the price asked for it in the shop.
C. The price of the item paid by the retailer is far less than the cost asked for it in the shop.
D. The price of the item paid by the retailer is far less than the price asked for it in the shop.

Answer [   ]

23.
A. Have you ever visited to the United States?
B. Have you ever be to the United States?
C. Have you ever visit the United States?
D. Have you ever visited the United States?

Answer [   ]

24.
A. He died of hunger while his father died from the wounds received in battle.
B. He died from hunger while his father died from the wounds received by battle.
C. He died by hunger while his father died from the wounds received in battle.
D. He died of hunger while his father died of the wounds received by battle.

Answer [   ]

25.
A. How frequently do you going to the gym?
B. How frequently are you going to the gym?
C. How frequently do you go to the gym?
D. How frequently does you go to the gym?

Answer [   ]

26.
A. I asked to say what you wanted and you said this is the only one that you liked.
B. I asked you to say what you wanted and you said this is the only that you liked.
C. I asked to tell me what you wanted and you said this is the only one that you liked.
D. I asked you to tell me what you wanted and you said this is the only one that you liked.

Answer

27.
A. They has been working so hard to close the deal.
B. They have been working so hard to close the deal.
C. They has worked so hard to close the deal.
D. They been working so hard to close the deal.

Answer

28.
A. She got them down from the top shelf where she always kept them so he could see what they were made of.
B. She got them down from the top shelf where she always put them so he could see what they were made of.
C. She got them down from the top shelf where she always kept them so he could see what they were made from.
D. She got them down from the top shelf where she always keep them so he could see what they were made from.

Answer

29.
A. Between them the childs shared the only pair of scissors.
B. Between them the children shared the scissors.
C. Between them the child shared the only scissor.
D. Between them the children shared the scissor.

Answer

30.

A. When in polite company, to establish your wishes I would ask, do you want to do something?

B. When in polite company, to establish your wishes I would ask, do you like to do something?

C. When in polite company, to establish your wishes I would ask, do you would like to do something?

D. When in polite company, to establish your wishes I would ask, do you would want to do something?

Answer _____

31.

A. The movie is due to begin presently; I hope it will be as good as the one we saw before two weeks.

B. The film is due to commence at present; I hope it will be as good as the one we saw two weeks ago.

C. The documentary is due to start just now; I hope it will be as good as the one we saw two weeks ago.

D. The motion picture will begin presently; I hope it will be as good as the one we saw two weeks ago.

Answer _____

32.

A. He had so many manuscripts and they were covered in so many dust.

B. He had so much papers and they were covered in so much dust.

C. He had so many paperbacks and they were covered in so much dust.

D. He had so much books but they were covered in many dust.

Answer _____

33.
A. My elder sister is elder than my only brother.
B. My elder sister is older than my only brother.
C. My older sister is older than my only brother.
D. My older sister is elder than my only brother.

Answer [   ]

34.
A. The prescription stated that one dose was to be taken every day but the patient found it too bitter to swallow.
B. The prescription stated that one dose was to be taken each day but the patient found it much bitter to swallow.
C. The prescription stated that one dose was to be taken every day but the patient found it very bitter to swallow.
D. The prescription stated that one dose was to be taken each day but the patient found it too bitter to swallow.

Answer [   ]

35.
A. The original is so different to the sequel but both films are guilty of sentimentalism.
B. The original is so different than the sequel but both films are guilty for sentimentalism.
C. The original is so different from the sequel but both films are guilty of sentimentalism.
D. The original is so different to the sequel but both films are guilty for sentimentalism.

Answer [   ]

36.
A. A bull market is a prolonged period of rise in stock prices.
B. A bull market is a prolonged period of risen stock price.
C. A bull market is a prolonged period of rising stock prices.
D. A bull market is a prolonged period of rises in stock price.

Answer [   ]

37.
A. She asked, does the cat enjoy visiting to the vet? He answered, she does not enjoy these kind of things.
B. She asked, does the cat enjoy visit to the vet? He answered, she does not enjoy this kind of things.
C. She asked, does the cat enjoy visits to the vet? He answered, she does not like things of this kind.
D. She asked, does the cat enjoy visits to the vet? He answered, she does not like these kind of things.

Answer [   ]

38.
A. All of us are convinced that all is well.
B. All of us is convinced that all is well.
C. All of us are convinced that all be well.
D. All of us is convinced that all are well.

Answer [   ]

39.
A. We had a really lovely meal and after we went home, where we found the front door opened.
B. We had a really lovely meal and afterwards we went home, where we found the front door open.
C. We had a really lovely meal and after we went home, where we found the front door open.
D. We had a really lovely meal and afterwards we went home, where we found the front door opened.

Answer [   ]

40.
A. What are you thinking will happen?
B. What do you thinking will happen?
C. What you think will happen?
D. What do you think will happen?

Answer [   ]

End of test.

Test 5. Reading comprehension and critical reasoning

This test comprises 14 passages and 42 questions and you are allowed 60 minutes in which to attempt them. Each passage is followed by a series of questions or statements and it is your task to answer the questions or statements by referring only to the contents of the passage. In every case you must indicate if the statement is true, false or that you cannot tell if the statement is true or false. To indicate your answer, write true, false or cannot tell in the answer box provided.

Work without interruption and complete the test in one continuous period.

If you cannot get to the solution of a question then it is worth guessing, but only as a last resort. Remember that to do well in a test you have to try hard.

Do not turn the page until you are ready to begin.

Passage 1

There was considerable concern expressed by biochemists in 2002 when news emerged that traces of Acrylamide were found in a great many food stuffs, including daily basics such as bread, breakfast cereals and potato and cheese products. Acrylamide is widely found in many processed foods but it is also created during home cooking, in fact whenever sugar, found in so many foods, is heated and browns. Blood tests showed that it was present in high concentrations in the vast majority of people in the Western world. The few animal studies that had taken place suggested that Acrrylamide is a carcinogen, but little was known about the toxicological consequences of ingesting the chemical daily and at the levels found in the general population. An urgent search began to establish what risk it posed to public health and how it might be removed from or reduced in food.

1. It can be inferred from the passage that even at trace levels if digested Acrylamide is toxic.
    True   False   Cannot tell
                                        Answer [   ]

2. The author of the passage would most likely disagree that many of the questions posed in the passage are now close to being answered.
    True   False   Cannot tell
                                        Answer [   ]

3. The likelihood of a potential health risk from the ingestion of Acrylamide would increase if it were found that, unlike in previous food scares, the option of removing from the shelves all foodstuffs in which it was present was not available because it is so widespread that there would be hardly anything left.
    True   False   Cannot tell
                                        Answer [   ]

Passage 2

The prime minister described climate change as the greatest long-term challenge facing the human race. In 1997 he committed Britain to cutting emissions of carbon dioxide by 20 per cent, with 2010 set as the date by which this reduction was to be achieved. This target was beyond the Kyoto target to reduce emissions and was self-imposed. Unfortunately, after initial success, progress towards the target slowed then stopped, and since 2002 carbon dioxide emissions have risen slightly. In 2005 the government admitted the obvious by conceding that the 20 per cent by 2010 target would not be realized. Some of the reasons are beyond the government's control. Very high prices for natural gas have in recent years meant that energy companies are switching to burning more and dirtier coal. Economic growth has exceeded expectations and resulted in higher than forecast levels of emissions. The government must also take a share of the blame. There has been a whole raft of reports, recommendations and policies directed at countering the causes of climate change. However, few of these initiatives are aimed at cutting emissions or providing incentives to change polluting behaviour. Instead, they largely fall into the category of raising awareness.

4. Britain will fail to realize its self-imposed target of a 20 per cent reduction by 2010 but will achieve the lower Kyoto target.
    True   False   Cannot tell

                                 Answer   ☐

5. The passage states that emissions would be lower than the current level if the British government had adopted more radical policies to counter carbon emissions.
    True   False   Cannot tell

                                 Answer   ☐

6. The passage follows events chronologically.
    True   False   Cannot tell

                                        Answer

Passage 3

A cross-party committee of MPs proposed a compromise in an
effort to resolve the stand-off over the reform of the rules on
political donations. It stated that political parties should volun-
tarily agree a limit to donations from individuals, companies or
trade unions, set lower spending limits for elections, increase the
transparency of party finances, and vote to increase taxpayers'
support. The idea behind putting a ceiling on donations is to
reduce the party's dependency on gifts from big organizations or
wealthy individuals. There is agreement over the need for greater
transparency and action that will prevent further loss of public
confidence in the political establishment, because of the
appearance of money buying power and influence.

7. It can be inferred from the passage that there is already a state
    subsidy paid towards political parties.
    True   False   Cannot tell

                                        Answer

8. The second sentence of the passage states the details of the
    stand-off between the political parties.
    True   False   Cannot tell

                                        Answer

9. There is nothing in the passage that suggests that the major
    issues that remain unresolved between the parties relate to
    whether or not to cap all donations and whether or not to
    apply spending limits on both local and national elections.
    True   False   Cannot tell

                                        Answer

Passage 4

'The Party of Regions' took 32 per cent of the vote, the block of parties led by Yulia Tymoshenko polled 22 per cent, 'Our Ukraine Party' secured 14 per cent and 'The Socialists' trailed with 3 per cent. The result means that the next government of the Ukraine is likely to be a coalition. A union between the parties led by Tymoshenko and 'Our Ukraine Party' seems least likely given that Tymoshenko was sacked from a ministerial post and split from the 'Our Ukraine Party' to run her election campaign on the platform of anti-corruption. Many commentators describe the electrical punishment dished out to the President and leader of the 'Our Ukraine Party', Mr Yushchenko, as expected. The newly established and largely free press played its part in bringing about the result and the parliamentary elections were by common agreement the freest so far.

10. The leader of the block of parties that polled 22 per cent of the vote is a woman.

    True   False   Cannot tell

                                    Answer   [   ]

11. It can be inferred from the passage that the election failed to produce an outright winner.

    True   False   Cannot tell

                                    Answer   [   ]

12. Tymoshenko was sacked by Yushchenko.

    True   False   Cannot tell

                                    Answer   [   ]

Passage 5

The science of laterality – the study of mental functions and the side of the brain from which they originate – was advanced recently by research that found that around 30 per cent of dogs were either left- or right-pawed and the remainder were ambidextrous. The research became of commercial interest when it was realized that the dogs that showed no preference for left or right were more likely to react badly to loud noises such as fireworks or thunderstorms. Such behaviour makes a dog unsuitable for a career sniffing out drugs or guiding the blind. As things stand, one in every two dogs fails the training programmes for these roles because of an intolerance of loud noise.

13. In relation to dogs, the term 'ambidextrous' can be taken to mean that they showed no preference as to which paw they use.

    True   False   Cannot tell

                                     Answer   [   ]

14. The case made in the passage would be strengthened if an intolerance to loud noise were manifest in dogs before they began training for careers as guides for the blind or to sniff out drugs.

    True   False   Cannot tell

                                     Answer   [   ]

15. The commercial interest mentioned in the passage can be taken to relate to a hope that a test of paw preference will improve the selection process by which dogs are chosen for these careers.

    True   False   Cannot tell

                                     Answer   [   ]

Passage 6

Rural isolation occurs when communities are left without access to essential economic and social components of modern life. Large tracts of the countryside have only one bus a week and there are many villages that are served by a single shop. It is easy to understand why residents feel betrayed if it closes. If that shop is also the local post office – the place in which, traditionally, pensions and state benefits are paid – then people often feel that the death knell of their community has been sounded. The UK has over 14,000 rural post offices, almost all located in community shops, and it is planned that 2,500 will close. They will be selected on the basis of commercial viability. Mobile post offices, internet services and the payment of benefits directly into claimants' bank accounts are proposed as a replacement for this vital national network.

16. To describe rural isolation is the main theme of the passage.
    True   False   Cannot tell

                                        Answer [   ]

17. The author would agree that public transport, government services and shops are examples of essential economic and social components of modern life.
    True   False   Cannot tell

                                        Answer [   ]

18. The author would agree that when a post office is closed and that post office is based in a community shop then it too will close.
    True   False   Cannot tell

                                        Answer [   ]

Passage 7

In northern communities it is not just shift-workers or long-distance flyers who find their daily life out of phase with the natural sleep–wake/light–dark cycle. In winter in those high latitudes most workers and school children get up hours before sunrise. They rely on heavy curtains in the summer months to darken a room from the evening sun so that they can sleep. It is not just the sleep–wake rhythm that is affected; blood pressure, body temperature, reaction times, appetite and levels of alertness all follow a daily cycle and are all synchronized with light and dark. Doctors recognize that a mismatch between our busy schedules and the hours of light and darkness leads to increases in many disorders. Weight gain, gastrointestinal complaints and depression are the most common. We seem the least seasonally sensitive of all species, even when you take into account the fact that we evolved in the tropics and many tropical animals exhibit fewer seasonal variations in behaviour.

19. It can be inferred from the passage that all animals (except for humans) dramatically adapt their behaviour to suit the seasons.

    True   False   Cannot tell

                                  Answer [   ]

20. The question of why many tropical animals exhibit fewer seasonal variations in behaviour is answered in the passage.

    True   False   Cannot tell

                                  Answer [   ]

21. The author would disagree that it is only people who live in northern latitudes who find their daily life out of phase with the light–dark cycle.

    True   False   Cannot tell

                                  Answer [   ]

Passage 8

Sales of 4×4s (vehicles in which the transmission is delivered through all four wheels) have slumped and existing owners face significant losses should they decide to sell. Environmental groups are happy to take responsibility for the change in fortunes and have campaigned vigorously against the vehicles. Government has suggested that drivers of the most polluting cars will be penalized with extra taxes. The high running cost was already starting to deter people from buying them. One of the reasons people opted to buy a 4×4 is their impressive passenger safety record.

22. The environmentalist campaign against 4×4s would be undermined if US research were to suggest that passengers in small cars are 50 times more likely to die in a head-on collision with another car than the passengers in a 4×4.

    True   False   Cannot tell

                                      Answer   [   ]

23. A basic assumption of the passage is that 4×4 vehicles are less fuel efficient than older large estates, saloons and people carriers.

    True   False   Cannot tell

                                      Answer   [   ]

24. Second-hand values of these cars have dropped significantly.

    True   False   Cannot tell

                                      Answer   [   ]

Passage 9

In 2003, after rising for two decades, new cases of breast cancer started to fall. Part of the reason for the rise in the incidence of the disease was the expansion of screening campaigns and an aging population. The sharp fall in the number of cases has been associated with an equally sharp fall in the number of women giving up hormone replacement therapy. The fall was highest amongst women aged between 50 and 69 who were more likely to have previously been receiving the therapy. Following detailed analysis of the available data and after adjustments were made for the aging population, the speed and rate of the fall in diagnosed cases came as a welcome surprise.

25. It was a surprise that the number of new cases should fall.
    True   False   Cannot tell

                                    Answer   [   ]

26. It would be wrong to deduce from the passage that screening started around 1982.
    True   False   Cannot tell

                                    Answer   [   ]

27. The link between the fall in cases of breast cancer and the fall in women taking hormone replacements is contingent.
    True   False   Cannot tell

                                    Answer   [   ]

Passage 10

It is possible that when our forbears looked skywards and saw the heavenly bodies they believed them to be the size they appear. In any event, the ancient mind did not seem to share our need to represent in two dimensions the illusion of depth. Any graphic method applied to a flat surface that successfully conveys the impressions of spatial extension is said to provide perspective. For example, if parallel lines are shown to converge and objects at a distance are depicted as smaller, then the impression of depth is achieved. These are ways an artist can create the illusion of perspective. A pair of railway lines represented as converging to a point on the horizon is perhaps the most striking example.

28. The author would agree that a forbear who painted the moon as it appears may not have needed to create the impression of spatial extension for his picture to be representational.
    True   False   Cannot tell

    Answer [   ]

29. It can be inferred from the passage that the painting of ancient Egypt lacks the illusion of perspective.
    True   False   Cannot tell

    Answer [   ]

30. Two methods are described through which an impression of depth on a flat surface can be created.
    True   False   Cannot tell

    Answer [   ]

Passage 11

Half of all the world's wealth is now held by 2 per cent of the world's population. There are estimated to be 500 dollar billionaires and over half a billion dollar millionaires. At the other end of the spectrum, the poorest half of the world's adult population cannot lay claim to even 1 per cent of global wealth. Per capita wealth was lowest in the Republic of Congo and estimated at $180 per person. Such inequality means that, for example, whole populations can never realistically aspire to own the land they work or the modest home in which they have lived for generations. Collectively, the citizens of North America, Europe and a few Asia Pacific countries hold 90 per cent of global wealth. But even within these wealth zones there is inequality. The United

States came top as the most unequal nation, while Japan and China had some of the lowest levels of inequality.

31. The author would not agree that wealth is largely the monopoly of people living in North America, Europe and a few Asia Pacific countries.

    True   False   Cannot tell

                                  Answer [   ]

32. There are poor people in every nation, so the passage can be criticized for making the mistaken assumption that the world's poor all live in certain countries.

    True   False   Cannot tell

                                  Answer [   ]

33. Such inequity between the rich and poor creates enormous tension.

    True   False   Cannot tell

                                  Answer [   ]

Passage 12

The immaculate white porcelain suddenly fell from vogue, to be replaced by painted porcelain. What was to become known as 'blue and white ware' because of its blue coloured designs over a white background, was greatly in demand for the export markets and used the newly discovered and imported Persian cobalt as an underglazing paint. So great was this trade that the plates and dishes decorated with dragons, phoenixes and flowers graced many European homes and featured in contemporary still-life paintings and portraits. In time the style evolved to include red, yellow and green overgrazes applied over blue outlines. Increasingly, designs depicted symbols of well-being such as groups of children, sages or animals.

34. The passage describes the development of Chinese ceramics.

True   False   Cannot tell

Answer [   ]

35. It can be deduced from the passage that painted porcelain became more popular than its predecessor.

True   False   Cannot tell

Answer [   ]

36. Persian cobalt gives porcelain a rich emerald-toned green colour.

True   False   Cannot tell

Answer [   ]

Passage 13

There are 150,000 criminals who have been convicted, have served a period in prison and been released early to be supervised in the community by the government's probation service. A small proportion while on probation commit further offences, including very serious crimes. Offenders on probation have been convicted of over 100 murders and a further 37 have been convicted of attempted murder. Critics point to the current automatic early release scheme that allows offenders to walk free after completing only a small fraction of their full sentence, as the cause of the current situation. The probation service responds by pointing out that any offending by people under their supervision is of great concern, but that the incidence of offenders who commit serious offences while on probation is low, with only 0.2 per cent of offenders being convicted of very serious crimes while on probation.

37. In the context of the passage, the term 'very serious crime' can be taken to mean murder or attempted murder.

True   False   Cannot tell

Answer [   ]

38. A premise of the passage is that the probation service is failing to properly supervise dangerous criminals.

True   False   Cannot tell

Answer [   ]

39. Whatever the probation service might say, 100 murders would not have occurred if it were not for the early release scheme.

True   False   Cannot tell

Answer [   ]

Passage 14

The leaders of a society might argue they have abolished poverty if they ensure that no citizens are homeless or starving. In developed Western societies, few would accept so narrow a definition. They are very likely to add further indicators such as the level of income, the standard of housing, the quality of diet, and access to everyday commodities such as heating, running hot water, a bath and a washing machine. The list soon grows from items essential to support life to include things that a society views as impracticable to be without. It is clear, therefore, that most people do not mean absolute poverty when they use the term, but something much more relative and dependent on the society in which they live. Because for most people poverty is a relative concept, its abolition is much more difficult. Poverty ends up being defined in terms of people who live on a percentage of the median income.

40. A hundred years ago people would have included in their definition of poverty many of the items listed in the passage as indicators of poverty in developed Western societies.

True   False   Cannot tell

Answer _____

41. If poverty is defined in terms of people who live on a percentage of the median income, then the number of people classed as in poverty could increase not because people are poorer but because they are not becoming richer as fast as the majority in their society.

True   False   Cannot tell

Answer _____

42. Absolute poverty would be cured if the poorest in society were fed, clothed and housed.

True   False   Cannot tell

Answer _____

End of test.

An interpretation of your score in the practice tests

A score over 30

If you face a graduate-level psychometric test such as GMAT, LSAT, the Civil Service Fast Stream, or the Graduate Battery of SHL, or are applying for an oversubscribed position or course where a high cut-off mark will be used, then this is the only category of score that you should be content with.

Your score suggests a high level of ability and confidence in verbal reasoning. You have demonstrated sustained concentration and an ability to work quickly and under pressure.

Concentrate the remaining time you have for further practice on material relevant to other aspects of the recruitment process that you face so that you can be sure you can perform to this high standard in all aspects of the challenge.

A score of 25 or above

This is a good score, especially if you secured it in Test 5. In the real test, the bulk of candidates are likely to score somewhere in this category. Your score may well be sufficient to get you through to the next stage of most recruitment processes, but it will depend on the number of other candidates and vacancies and your precise position in relation to the performance of others.

If you found you did not have sufficient time to complete all the questions, speed up. You might try risking getting a few more wrong because you do not double-check your answers, but this way you will have more time to attempt more questions. Alternatively, practise at better managing your time during the test and avoid spending too long on questions that you find difficult.

If you found it hard to maintain the level of concentration demanded by the practice tests, this is entirely normal. At the end of tests like these you should feel completely wiped out! If you don't, you're not making the required effort. Remember that even a very able candidate, if he or she is to do well in tests like these, has to try very hard. Make yourself keep going right until you hear 'Put your pencil down' or the clock runs out of time on the computer screen.

Undertake more practice and see if you can improve that bit more. If you can, you might succeed in pulling yourself further ahead of the majority of candidates and be more sure of a positive result.

A score below 25

Go over the questions that you got wrong and the explanations, and try to work out where you went wrong. It helps to get someone else's opinion. Such a review will greatly assist you to understand the demands of these types of test.

Once you have completed a thorough review, take a break, overnight preferably, and get yourself into a really determined mindset. Find a quiet space and enough time and take the next test, only this time really go for it and practise what you learnt from the last test; prove to yourself that you can do better. You might well be pleasantly surprised with the next result. If you manage a better score on your next attempt then you have made an important discovery. You have realized that you have what it takes to do well in these tests and you have found what you have to do to do well in these tests.

Now set aside a quite significant amount of time for further practice. Seek out other titles in the Kogan Page testing series containing these sorts of questions, and make it a habit to read a quality newspaper every day and economic and political weekly magazines.

Take encouragement from the fact that with practice you can show dramatic improvements in your score. In time you will gain further in confidence, accuracy and speed. It will take time, but if the opportunity towards which you are working is something you really want, then go for it. You have already begun the process of dramatically improving your score, so take encouragement. The vast majority of candidates will discover the hard way that they need more practice, by failing a real test. You are already ahead of them, so track down sufficient practice material on which to work, get started in plenty of time, and you will go on to pass something you might otherwise have failed.

Answers and detailed explanations

Chapter 3. 150 Warm-up questions

Word link: opposites

1. tighten
2. acquit
3. tiny
4. severe *Explanation*: in architecture the opposite of a highly ornate style is a severe one without decoration.
5. muted
6. spurn *Explanation*: spurn means to refuse, which is an opposite of one meaning of accommodate – 'the unexpected visitors were accommodated/spurned'.
7. composure
8. effervescent *Explanation*: in the sense of a still drink the opposite is a carbonated or effervescent drink.
9. self-conscious *Explanation*: narcissistic means self-centred and the closest opposite is someone who is self-conscious.
10. elated *Explanation*: the news galled him, the opposite of elated him.
11. formula *Explanation*: a cipher is a code and a formula a type of answer or solution.
12. unbiased

13. lukewarm reader   *Explanation*: 'biblio' means book, while a word ending in 'phile' means to love.
14. authenticate
15. grimace   *Explanation*: to grimace is to frown.
16. excitable   *Explanation*: 'phlegmatic' means calm and unflappable.
17. considerable   *Explanation*: 'scant' means little or small, so the opposite is considerable.
18. less than half of something   *Explanation*: to say something is the lion's share is to say it is most or the larger part.
19. make the grade   *Explanation*: 'founder' can mean the originator of, say, a company, or to fail. Of the suggested answers 'make the grade' is the closest opposite to this second meaning.
20. primary   *Explanation*: 'subsidiary' means subordinate and the opposite is primary. 'Principal' would also be an opposite (but not principle); 'primarily' means for the most part or mainly.
21. inaccurate   *Explanation*: 'faithful' is used to mean loyal and accurate; in the second usage 'inaccurate' is the opposite.
22. impose   *Explanation*: 'lift' has many uses, one of which is 'to revoke' and the opposite of this is to 'impose'.
23. transparent
24. refute
25. enable
26. narrow   *Explanation*: 'emphatic' has two meanings: vigorous and decisive, and the opposite of the second of these is 'narrow', ie they won by a narrow/emphatic margin.
27. verbose   *Explanation*: 'laconic' means to be brief or unforthcoming.
28. multifaceted
29. spartan   *Explanation*: the opposite of the adjective 'opulent' is 'spartan', while the opposite of the noun 'opulence' is 'poverty'.
30. real   *Explanation*: 'nominal' means either tiny or in name only, and the opposite of the second of these is 'real'.

Word link: synonyms

31. C and E, iconoclast and critic   *Explanation*: 'iconify' is a computer term meaning to reduce to an icon; iconology is the study of visual imagery. An iconoclast is a critic or sceptic.
32. A and F, inopportune and inconvenient
33. B and E, monotonous and unchallenging
34. B and D, postponement and deferral   *Explanation*: 'postponement' means to defer something, not necessarily to reschedule or shelve it.
35. C and F, hawk and retail   *Explanation*: another way to say to 'retail' or 'sell' something is to 'hawk' it.
36. A and F, duty and toll   *Explanation*: when we refer to a tax as a duty another word for it is a 'toll'.
37. C and E, scepticism and uncertainty
38. A and D, descend and plunge   *Explanation*: in a bear market or during a recession markets may plunge, but only 'descend' means plunge.
39. B and F, calamitous and cataclysmic
40. A and F, elucidation and clarification
41. C and D, elicit and evoke
42. B and E, amalgamation and consolidation
43. A and E, meritorious and exemplary
44. C and E, flexible and pliable   *Explanation*: flexitime is the daily working style where hours are flexible.
45. B and D, preference and penchant
46. A and D, stigma and shame
47. C and E, incongruent and disparate   *Explanation*: 'disparate' means dissimilar and so is closer in meaning to 'incongruent' than 'illogical'.
48. B and D, equivocate and waver
49. C and F, withstand and weather
50. C and E, affirmative and absolutely
51. A and D, wholly and unconditionally   *Explanation*: 'wholly' and 'unconditionally' are closer in meaning than 'momentarily' and 'temporarily'.

52. C and D, stable and static
53. B and F, confident and buoyant
54. B and E, overt and brazen
55. C and D, elucidate and clarify
56. A and E, rough and broad
57. B and D, annul and rescind
58. A and F, scarcely and hardly
59. C and D, footloose and roaming *Explanation*: 'footsie' is a popular name for the FT-SE 100 index. A 'footer' is a statement at the bottom of a document.
60. B and F, empathetic and commiserative *Explanation*: to be emphatic (categorical) is not the same as to emphasize (to stress).

Find the new word

61. easy
62. soft
63. only and calm
64. tear
65. room
66. user and once
67. area and rear
68. zero
69. test and text
70. stow and town
71. tape
72. whey and year
73. vein and shop
74. cell, icon and lace
75. bias and inch
76. echo
77. pawn
78. deed
79. bait

80. acre
81. imam   *Explanation*: a leader in the Muslim faith
82. life
83. role
84. neap and seed
85. lead and tick
86. veto
87. ally
88. mate
89. life
90. dyno   *Explanation*: 'dyno' is a climbing term that means a quick move across a rock face.

Word swap

91. pans and knives
92. each and every
93. guest and name
94. actual and written
95. fact and that
96. traffic and winds
97. spiders and people
98. problems and aspects
99. communicate and benefit
100. essential and current
101. fixed and rung
102. hasn't and has
103. professional and dependent
104. (second) no and zero
105. subsistence and nomadic
106. which and has
107. standard and existence
108. bad and good
109. colourful and expensive
110. (first) problem and place
111. share and consume
112. secret and aerodynamics
113. international and world's
114. (first) emits and unlike
115. afternoon and midday
116. enthusiastic and since
117. astronomical and innovative
118. landscape and inspiration
119. amplification and acronym
120. father and model

Sentence sequence

121. CDBA   122. CDAB   123. BCAD
124. DCBA   125. DCAB   126. ADCB

127. BDCA	128. DACB	129. CDAB
130. CADB	131. DACB	132. ABDC
133. BDCA	134. CBAD	135. DBCA
136. BDCA	137. CBAD	138. DCAB
139. DBAC	140. BDCA	141. DBCA
142. CDAB	143. CADB	144. ADBC
145. DBCA	146. DCBA	147. BDAC
148. ADCB	149. CDBA	150. CDAB

Chapter 4. 100 English usage questions

Correctly complete the sentence

1. C *Explanation*: the incidental clause 'a seaside town' requires enclosing commas to separate it from the main thought in the sentence. We can correctly say either 'World War I' or the 'First World War' but both should start with upper-case letters.

2. A *Explanation*: ID should be in upper case and we use commas to itemize, but conclude the list with 'and' (we could also conclude with 'plus').

3. D *Explanation*: it is incorrect but common to use a comma when the sentence needs a linking word (alternatively we could use a semicolon to link the clauses).

4. A *Explanation*: we could adopt either structure for our lists but after a colon we only start a word with an upper case letter in the case of proper nouns.

5. C *Explanation*: a colon can be used to introduce a conclusion but we would not follow it with an upper case H in he; 'where' is incorrect as it refers to position or place, while 'were' is the past tense of 'be'.

6. B   *Explanation*: it would be impossible for a house to fly into a kitchen, so to avoid confusion the words are united, in some cases with a hyphen, but in this case by joining the words.

7. A   *Explanation*: both ill-timed and three-quarters are hyphenated.

8. D   *Explanation*: we use the upper case when we refer to a named road, square, avenue, etc and the lower case to refer to an unnamed road, square or avenue.

9. B   *Explanation*: the possessive apostrophe is normally placed before the 's', but in the case of plural words that end in 's', such as employees, then the apostrophe follows the 's' – employees'.

10. B   *Explanation*: we place 'an' before words that begin with a vowel sound (including most of those with a silent 'h'); we would say 'one' rather than 'a' slice to emphasis the choice of items.

11. A   *Explanation*: before a singular noun we say 'the whole' rather than 'all' or 'all the' and after 'almost' we prefer 'every' rather than 'each' to emphasis that we are referring to a group of things (in this case, days).

12. C   *Explanation*: when a noun is uncountable we would use no article or 'some', but when there is a negative meaning as in the case of the second clause, we would use 'any' or 'anything'.

13. A   *Explanation*: 'they've' is the abbreviation for 'they have', while 'who's' is incorrect as it means 'who is' or 'who has'.

14. D   *Explanation*: the incidental clause needs enclosing commas to separate it.

15. B   *Explanation*: the sentence needs a linking word between the clauses and it is incorrect to use a comma.

16. C   *Explanation*: to make sense the sentence needs the first reference to weeks to mean quite a large number; in the case of the second gap we use 'less than' when the noun is uncountable and 'fewer' when it is countable.

17. A *Explanation*: the only suggestion that produces a sensible answer is A. 'Whom' is used in the more formal situation rather than 'who', and it is preferred immediately after a preposition.
18. D *Explanation*: questions marks are used only when there is a direct question and not in the case of the first reference to a question, which is indirect.
19. D *Explanation*: words beginning 'pre' are rarely hyphenated, unless it improves the sense, while words beginning 'self' usually are.
20. C *Explanation*: in the first space we could omit a word or use 'ones' (to go with 'these'); in the second space we need 'one' to indicate the single artichoke to which we are referring.
21. A *Explanation*: if we say that we have more or less of an adjective, then we use gradable adverbs that quantify adjectives, but in the case of an adjective that is ungradeable we can only emphasize its absolute state and not its degree.
22. C *Explanation*: we can say 'due to' or 'owing to' after a degree adverb, but we prefer 'due to' when the statement is categorical.
23. C *Explanation*: 'although' and 'whilst' suggest the contrast between being the cleverest but failing the most exams; 'even' is incorrect as it means may or may not be, in this context.
24. A *Explanation*: 'delegates' are a countable group and so we use the plural 'number' rather than the uncountable singular 'amount'. The verb tense of the sentence requires the past tense.
25. C *Explanation*: the possessive apostrophe is not required in the case of 'bosses' as there is nothing to indicate as belonging to them. In the case of the seamstress, we need the possessive apostrophe which is added before an extra 's'.
26. D *Explanation*: 'proficiency' is the noun form of 'proficient', while in this context the past form 'had' is correct; 'did' would be correct if, for example, the sentence read 'he worked hard every day to improve his Italian but to hear him speak you would not think he did'.

27. B   *Explanation*: the sentence could correctly start with 'in order to', 'to' or 'so as to' but not 'so to'; but only 'so as' correctly completes the sentence, making suggested answer B the only correct one.

28. D   *Explanation*: 'neither' is followed by 'nor' and 'either' by 'or'.

29. A   *Explanation*: when the noun 'important' is used as an uncountable, as in this case, it does not have an article.

30. B   *Explanation*: 'I'd' is the abbreviation for 'I had' or 'I would'; 'wouldn't' is the abbreviation for 'would not'.

31. D   *Explanation*: words beginning in 'un' are not usually hyphenated, while those beginning with 'non' usually are.

32. B   *Explanation*: the assignment is not her last as another awaits her, so we say 'latest'; 'lose' means 'lost', while 'loose' means in this context 'set free'.

33. D   *Explanation*: 'principle' is correct in this context and means adherence to a moral code ('principal' means main idea or chief person); we can correctly refer back to someone with 'their', 'them' or 'they'.

34. C   *Explanation*: 'where' refers to a location or other relationship and 'whereby' means 'by which' ('where' could be used in both positions but this option is not offered).

35. A   *Explanation*: we say we have an interest *in* something and an admiration *for* someone.

36. D   *Explanation*: 'incidence' is singular, so we say 'correlates with' not 'correlates to'.

37. A   *Explanation*: the sentence poses an indirect question, so a question mark is not required.

38. C   *Explanation*: for the sentence to make sense the message had to arrive after leaving for the meeting. B is wrong because the abbreviation for 'did not' is 'didn't'.

39. B   *Explanation*: we start a quote of direct speech with a capital and use the capital for the first letter of place names, even when they are used to name some other thing like a type of food.

40. A *Explanation*: we can start the sentence with 'No' (for emphasis) or 'Not a', but we would not start it with 'not any of them'; in this situation we prefer to say 'no one'.

Identify the correct sentence

41. B *Explanation*: we can correctly say 'round' or 'around' when referring to the distribution of something. We use 'know' when we are referring to something we have learnt; when we refer to something we can/could learn we use the expression 'get to know'.

42. B *Explanation*: to talk about the past we use 'if it had not been'; we would use 'were not' or 'was not' to refer to the present or future. We could correctly use the structure suggested in C, but the inclusion of 'been lost' confuses the intention – was Wellington at risk of being lost at Waterloo?

43. C *Explanation*: we can correctly say 'I feel like' to mean 'I want something', so all the sentences start correctly but only for people, animals and plants would we say 'male', otherwise we would use the term 'masculine'.

44. A *Explanation*: we correctly say 'farther' or 'further' when talking about distance but we say 'further' when we mean 'additional'.

45. D *Explanation*: only D is a complete sentence with an identified main clause.

46. A *Explanation*: we *bring* something or someone to the place of the speaker and *take* something or someone to another place.

47. C *Explanation*: we say 'down to' less important places such as the passage, which is less important that the (implied) room, and the country (when compared with the town). We say 'up to' more important places.

48. A *Explanation*: 'lose' means 'lost', while 'loose' means 'not tight'.

49. D *Explanation*: suggested answers A and B do not make sense (to say something would be to complain and to complain would necessarily involve saying something); C would be correct but should read 'it's' and not 'its'.

50. A *Explanation*: a metaphor involves applying a word or phrase to a subject to which it is not literally applicable, in this case the description of a capitalist as a parasite.

51. C *Explanation*: we prefer to say 'agree to' in recognition of our choice in the matter; we *cross* a desert, go *over* a hill, but walk *through* a forest.

52. D *Explanation*: we don't put adverbs between a verb and the object.

53. C *Explanation*: we say 'afraid' to mean 'sorry' when we say something negative or unwelcome, for example, 'I'm afraid it's going to rain tomorrow.' When we want to decline something politely we use the term 'afraid not'.

54. B *Explanation*: in this context it is correct to say 'apart from', 'except' or 'besides', but only B uses the correct 'born'.

55. A *Explanation*: we can use 'all' to mean 'everything', but only in the form of 'all that'.

56. B *Explanation*: 'hadn't hardly' and 'hadn't scarcely' both involve an unnecessary double negative. C is wrong because 'sale' is spelt 'sail'.

57. D *Explanation*: we borrow something from someone and lend someone something; we say 'borrowed' something so that we could do something.

58. B *Explanation*: we say *at* hours (at 3 o'clock) *in* the afternoon/evening, etc, *at* the weekend and *in* a month or year.

59. D *Explanation*: sarcasm uses mockery to convey contempt.

60. C *Explanation*: we use 'throughout' to say that something is in every part; 'it's' is the contraction of 'it is', while the possessive is 'its'.

61. A *Explanation*: we can use either 'you' or, rather formally, 'one'; however, we do not switch between them. In this example we cannot use 'you' as it is wrong to say 'you gets'.

62. B *Explanation*: the sentence requires everyone to help with finding both the culprit and the money, so 'everyone' must be placed where it applies generally.

63. C *Explanation*: 'kind' is singular and so requires agreement with 'trainer' rather than 'trainers', and it also requires the modifier 'this'.

64. A *Explanation*: when we refer to two objects we use 'between'; when there are more that two we use 'among'. To 'lie' is to recline, while to 'lay' is to lay something, so involving a reference to something, in this case the sheets.

65. D *Explanation*: we use the structure 'neither... nor' when there is a common position and in this case the verb matches the noun that precedes it.

66. B *Explanation*: when we construct a sentence with 'either/ or' we place the correlatives as close as possible to the subject to which they refer.

67. D *Explanation*: 'papers' are plural and so require the plural verb, while the request for the newspaper cuttings was singular, so it requires the singular verb.

68. A *Explanation*: 'trade federation' is a singular subject, so takes the singular 'has' rather than the plural 'have', and it is not a person, so we use 'its' rather than 'their'.

69. D *Explanation*: we can infer that there is a class of people who had previously challenged the chief executive and therefore in its correct form the sentence needs the demonstrative pronoun 'from those'.

70. C *Explanation*: the subject of the sentence 'is' a singular fact and so carries a singular verb, 'proves'.

71. A *Explanation*: suggested answers B and D do not make sense. The form of the sentence is the past conditional and it therefore requires the past perfect conditional, 'had not taken'.

72. B   *Explanation*: the causal link between the two fragments of the sentence leads us from the first to the second, so we use 'so' to make the link rather than the alternatives. Were the link the other way around then we would use 'because'.

73. A   *Explanation*: the sentence is in the past conditional, so needs the past perfect conditional clause.

74. D   *Explanation*: note that 'too' can mean in addition, like, also, as well and not very. We construct sentences usually with 'also' in mid position, while 'too' and 'as well' usually occur at the end of a clause. We would not correctly say the food was 'too well cooked'. We would not say something was 'too... as well'.

75. D   *Explanation*: 'number' refers to countable items, 'amount' refers to uncountable quantities. When making a comparison we say 'as... as' and not 'as... not'.

76. C   *Explanation*: something is either impossible or not and we avoid saying 'very impossible' or 'fairly impossible', but we do say 'quite impossible' for emphasis.

77. C   *Explanation*: an expression is a personification when human attributes are assigned to non-human things. In C money is said to talk, which is a personification.

78. D   *Explanation*: we use the same structure when constructing a sentence, so it is correct to say 'check' and 'double-check' or 'checking' and 'double-checking', but not to mix the structures. The correct verb tense for the sentence is determined by 'they had', which makes 'was time' correct.

79. A   *Explanation*: 'alternate' means 'every other', while 'alternative' means 'another'. 'All together' means 'everyone', while 'altogether' means 'completely'.

80. B   *Explanation*: the friend is a new one, so it is better to say that you made a new acquaintance.

81. D   *Explanation*: we say 'bread and butter', 'knife and fork' and 'hands and knees', and it is considered wrong to change the order. It is correct to say either 'you try to eat' or 'try and eat'.

82. C *Explanation*: 'affect' means influence, while 'effect' means cause, and in this case it is an influence affecting the resolve of the committee members, who are people, so referred to as 'they' rather than an object referred to as 'it'.

83. A *Explanation*: hyperbole is a description that is an over-exaggeration, and to say that someone would 'give the Earth' is an exaggeration as no one has the Earth to give.

84. D *Explanation*: a train moves *along* or *on* a track and passengers jump *off on to* the station platform.

85. B *Explanation*: to be cynical involves expressing the view that people are motivated by self-interest alone, and answer B most closely reflects this sentiment.

86. C *Explanation*: we do not start a sentence with 'Not any' but say 'No' instead; 'some expert' could be an expert in any field, while to say 'any expert' means it does not matter which – they will all agree. We say either 'could turn up any time' or 'will turn up some time'; both expressions are correct in this context.

87. D *Explanation*: 'into' makes clearer the action mother suggested. A and C are incorrect because 'like' should not be used as a conjunction (although it often incorrectly is).

88. C *Explanation*: a euphemism is when we substitute a polite word for one that may seem offensive or insensitive, and we often substitute 'passing away' for 'died'.

89. A *Explanation*: 'through' means to make a hole, 'though' means 'despite the fact'; we can correctly structure the sentence as 'although it was...' or 'foggy as it was...' or 'foggy though it was...' but we cannot correctly use the structure 'foggy as though it was'.

90. B *Explanation*: 'datum' is singular ('data' is the plural), so it is correct to say 'is'. The sentence needs 'it is' or its abbreviation 'it's' to read correctly.

91. D *Explanation*: the subject is computers and the object the world. In D the verb 'to run' directly transmits from the subject to the object.

92. D   *Explanation*: 'if' and 'would' cannot be placed together in the same clause; instead we use 'had'.

93. C   *Explanation*: because the sentence starts with 'anyone' we say 'they' rather than 'you' or 'she'.

94. D   *Explanation*: a simile involves drawing a comparison between two unlikely things and takes the form '...like' or 'as...'.

95. C   *Explanation*: in this context 'hopefully' means full of hope, and before it could make sense the sentence would need to read '... that he was full of hope that his team...'.

96. D   *Explanation*: we use 'at' when locating a precise position or group activity, but 'in' when the position is large like a town.

97. C   *Explanation*: 'at first' introduces a contrast, while 'first' is used to introduce an initial subject. 'Beside' means at the side, while 'besides' means as well as.

98. C   *Explanation*: a recidivist is a criminal who reoffends, so in the case of A and B it is unnecessary to describe the recidivist as criminal and as reoffending. C is correct because we say 'to try to' and not 'to try and'.

99. B   *Explanation*: a non-sequitur is a phrase or clause that does not follow locally from the previous phrase or clause. In the case of B the clause about sending the public back to school does not follow from the lack of trust.

100. A   *Explanation*: the sentence is in the past conditional tense, so needs the past perfect conditional clause.

Chapter 5. 100 True, false or cannot tell questions

1. False   *Explanation*: the passage states, 'The next time an astronaut walks there' but the subject of this statement is not walking to the moon.
2. Cannot tell   *Explanation*: the passage states that the station will be engaged in scientific research and that its most ambitious task will be a manned mission to Mars, but we are not told of the station's principal (most important) objective.
3. False   *Explanation*: one reason given in the passage for the preference of this location is dependent on this assumption but the conclusion is not wholly dependent on this assumption because another reason given is the near continuous sunlight useful for the generation of solar power.
4. True   *Explanation*: the passage states that outside the cities people have no alternative but to use their cars; if these areas were served by an affordable public transport system then there would be an alternative.
5. Cannot tell   *Explanation*: the passage states that they (the people who live outside the cities) already pay among the highest petrol duties in the world but it does not stay whether or not they pay the same or a higher rate than those who live in the cities.
6. True   *Explanation*: the statement that the well-off driver will be able to continue driving while other drivers will not does assume that the new tax is sufficiently high to deter less-well-off car users.
7. False   *Explanation*: the passage states that cholera and the other identified diseases cause a great many deaths but not that cholera is a water-borne disease.
8. False   *Explanation*: the passage states that they make a significant contribution towards public health and that in the *British Medical Journal* they were voted the greatest medical breakthrough.

9. False *Explanation*: the second sentence states that water had always been the greatest vector of disease but not that it still is the greatest.

10. True *Explanation*: this is the meaning of the term 'gravy train'. Don't be tempted to answer 'cannot tell' just because the passage does not provide a definition of the term. You are expected to know the meaning of the words and terms used in these passages.

11. False *Explanation*: the committee's comments were directed towards the public sector, not the private sector.

12. Cannot tell *Explanation*: the passage reports an expensive waste but it is not quantified.

13. False *Explanation*: 'ambivalent' means unsure, but in the passage the author's attitude is confident and disapproving.

14. False *Explanation*: the passage states that pre-packed foods are expensive.

15. True *Explanation*: the author argues for fresh food prepared by ourselves and eaten together and against processed food eaten in a hurry; it is probable therefore that the author would agree with the fact stated in the question.

16. True *Explanation*: an explanation is an explanatory statement and the ultimate sentence in the passage is suitably explained in the question.

17. Cannot tell *Explanation*: while this is an observation that many of us would recognize, it is not a subject covered in the passage, so we must conclude that we cannot tell.

18. True *Explanation*: this is a reasonable statement of the principal point made in the passage.

19. True *Explanation*: it says in the passage that particles were found that are older than our sun, and therefore older than our solar system, and that they remain in deep space unchanged.

20. False *Explanation*: the passage does not comment on whether or not scientists were startled, so we know this statement to be untrue. (Note: had the questions not referred

to the passage and stated only that 'The findings startled scientists', then the answer would have been 'cannot tell'.)

21. True   *Explanation*: 'rebutted' means disproved and it is stated in the passage that scientists were able to use spectrometers and electron microscopes to identify the mineral and chemical compositions of the particles.

22. Cannot tell   *Explanation*: the passage makes no comment on the fears of parents.

23. Cannot tell   *Explanation*: the passage reports that boys spend more on sporting activities than girls, but it does not say whether or not there is a gender trend in food-related spending, so we cannot say if they devote a greater part of their non-food spending on this activity than girls.

24. True   *Explanation*: the passage states that children spent equal sums on mobile phones and charges, and activities and objects that could be classed as educational. Books can be classed as educational but they are not the only object that can be so classed and while the amount is equal to that spent on mobile phones the amount spent is not detailed.

25. False   *Explanation*: the passage uses the term 'trend' in reference to the increase in the number of workers paying the top rate of tax.

26. False   *Explanation*: the passage states that 1 million people now pay tax at the higher rate because of the link between increases in tax allowances and inflation. The remaining 2 million people now pay tax at the higher rate because wages have risen at a rate higher than general inflation.

27. True   *Explanation*: this is a reasonable summary of the cause of the trend described in the passage.

28. True   *Explanation*: the passage states that users of virtual communities freely share their own work and all our cultural outpourings should be free to share. From this it can be reasonably inferred that the author would agree with the statement made in the passage.

29. False   *Explanation*: the passage does in fact present an either/or scenario: either payment is extracted or cultural outpourings should be free to share. No balance between these two positions is considered.
30. False   *Explanation*: the term in the context of the passage means the right to be recognized and acknowledged as the author, not the father.
31. True   *Explanation*: the author identifies what he sees as failings in the status quo and in the last sentence states that the world 'needs mechanisms capable of better protecting' it.
32. False   *Explanation*: there is no reference to a revolution or anything that could be described as one, so this cannot be inferred from the passage.
33. False   *Explanation*: you do not need to know anything of liberal politics to answer this question and the question is not asking you to say whether or not the explanation of that tradition provided in the question is correct. You need simply take the description provided of that school and decide if the passage is consistent with it. The passage is arguing for the global community to be protected from the excesses of individual national interests, which is quite different from the view that it is the interests of the nation state that need protecting.
34 Cannot tell   *Explanation*: you cannot establish from the passage if the author believes the decision will establish or undermine the green credentials of the Commission.
35. True   *Explanation*: it is clear that some members are split – at least the environmental and industrial commissioners. The question does not ask if the Commission is split, which we cannot tell from the passage.
36. True   *Explanation*: a tautology is the unnecessary repetition within a statement of the same thing. In one statement of the passage it is said 'that is lowered annually, year on year', which is a tautology.
37. True   *Explanation*: it is stated in the passage that 'the majority of people including many teachers do not have a

sufficient grasp of the rules to realize that a mistake has been made' and from this we can infer that most people don't object to bad grammar as they would not realize it was bad and so could not object.

38. False   *Explanation*: you cannot infer this as it is clear from the passage that people who do not know the rules are perfectly capable of breaking them and producing written work that contains bad grammar.

39. Cannot tell   *Explanation*: the author refers to the irritation some feel, but no information is offered as to whether or not the author believes that grammar matters for reasons other than this.

40. False   *Explanation*: the passage describes January and February as the two warmest months worldwide, but these are only winter months in the northern hemisphere.

41. False   *Explanation*: the passages states that there were only two exceptions and China was not one of them, so we can infer that China *did* experience record temperatures.

42. Cannot tell   *Explanation*: we are not provided with the figures, so we cannot establish how the findings might have changed.

43. True   *Explanation*: the statement made in the question can be established as true because the passage describes it as the Eurozone, the countries mentioned are European and the data are described as downbeat or in other words disappointing.

44. True   *Explanation*: the passage states that no one now expects one and that retail, housing and manufacturing have slowed or are in decline.

45. False   *Explanation*: you cannot conclude from the passage that a cut will be made soon. The passage states 'the talk is of cuts, but for the time being anyway it is probably too early to say when a cut might be made'.

46. Cannot tell   *Explanation*: the passage does not comment directly on the feelings of children not included in the scheme, nor can it be inferred from the content of the passage.

47. False   *Explanation*: the passage states that a teacher in every school will lead on the project and rely on their peers to identify children, not the children themselves.
48. False   *Explanation*: that gifted children may not always behave themselves was given as a reason why the scheme may not succeed in identifying the really gifted or talented child rather than as a justification for the initiative.
49. False   *Explanation*: the case made in the passage is that Scandinavia is an egalitarian delight and that Greek men are the least reconstructed in Europe. If it were discovered that women want equality at home and for men to share domestic chores, then this would in fact support the case made in the passage, not weaken it.
50. False   *Explanation*: the purpose is to report the findings of a survey into who carries out domestic chores across Europe.
51. True   *Explanation*: it is possible that the statement is true.
52. Cannot tell   *Explanation*: it is possible that the researchers have identified the form of beneficial exercise but it is also possible that they have found only that exercise is a positive factor but not the specific type of exercise.
53. False   *Explanation*: we cannot identify for whom the passage was written but we can conclude that it was not intended more for the group of physically inactive people over the population in general.
54. True   *Explanation*: the phrase 'is held to be' allows for other views and so for the possibility of disagreement.
55. True   *Explanation*: the passage states that four of the best five schools are US-based and the European Glasgow School is the only non-US school.
56. Cannot tell   *Explanation*: from the passage we know Lynx came first, Stanford second and Harvard third, but we do not know if Glasgow was in fourth or fifth place, only that it was the only non-US school in the top five.
57. Cannot tell   *Explanation*: neither the criteria nor the mechanism for grading the schools is commented on in the passage.

58. False   *Explanation*: the passage offers two possible explanations for the increase: one is that more young children develop the condition, the other is that the increase is due to a marked improvement in diagnosis. The second of these reasons, if correct, does not support the conclusion that five times as many young people are developing the condition. The same number of children would have developed the illness but few would have been diagnosed.

59. False   *Explanation*: the passage allows for two possibilities if the cause is environmental. One is something new that is the cause, the other is that we have reduced exposure to something that was previously providing protection.

60. True   *Explanation*: this is a reasonable explanation of the increase in cases.

61. True   *Explanation*: this fact would weaken the case made in the passage because it is claimed that mosquitoes in Italy are associated with every type of water body.

62. True   *Explanation*: 'genera' is the plural form of 'genus'; you can tell this from the passage because the passage states there are six genera of mosquitoes.

63. False   *Explanation*: no information is provided on this point in the passage.

64. Cannot tell   *Explanation*: the passage states that the atlas includes the earliest known printed plan of a US city but it does not say if the illustrations of England and Wales are the first or in the form of maps.

65. False   *Explanation*: the term 'attributed' means that an object is regarded as 'belonging or appropriate to' a person's work.

66. True   *Explanation*: 'multifunctional' means that something fulfils several functions and the passage states that the atlas provides an illustration of a survey of England and Wales and the expedition of Sir Frances Drake to the West Indies and what is now the United States.

67. True   *Explanation*: The passage states that the system ranks substances according to the harm they cause, for example the cost to the state. It is reasonable therefore to conclude that a drug's rating reflects its prevalence.

68. False   *Explanation*: This is a subsidiary point; the main point is that alcohol and tobacco cause more harm than many illegal drugs.

69. True   *Explanation*: The passage states that cannabis is below alcohol and tobacco in the league and that tobacco is ranked tenth. From this we can infer that cannabis is placed in the lower half.

70. True   *Explanation*: the passage states that the information will include details of the parents' education.

71. False   *Explanation*: if this were true then the wealthy person who retired early would not need to disclose anything.

72. False   *Explanation*: 'veracity' means in this context accuracy and other synonyms including truthfulness and honesty.

73. True   *Explanation*: 'duped' means misled and the author does suggest that consumers are misled into believing that the meat is British when the packaging shows the British countryside and the content is called 'farmhouse'.

74. Cannot tell   *Explanation*: to judge the statement as either true or false we would need more information regarding what constitutes a treatment or process resulting in a substantial change.

75. False   *Explanation*: the passage leads the reader to the view that the labelling of food as a product of the country in which the processing took place should be stopped, not the processing itself.

76. False   *Explanation*: they would pay the highest band of charge on public transport too.

77. False   *Explanation*: the passage makes no reference to the length of the journeys and so it cannot be inferred that the charge would depend on the length as well as the time of the journey.

78. False   *Explanation*: the question highlights a valid flaw in the comparison but the flaw has no bearing on the effectiveness of the charge in terms of its impact on congestion at peak times.

79. False   *Explanation*: strictly speaking, you might answer true to this question, but these questions are about judgement and it must be judged that the author did not literally mean 60 per cent of all the world's population, so the correct answer is false.

80. True   *Explanation*: by using the examples of the iPod and Nokia phone the author of the passage does focus on highly successful examples.

81. True   *Explanation*: the passage is making the point that successful brands go deeper than a catchy name and memorable logo and include the shape, feel and sound.

82. Cannot tell   *Explanation*: the passage does not provide information about the proportion of global economic activity that the United States enjoys now or 30 years ago. It only says that the US economy does not have the same clout or influence as it used to have; it could be the same size.

83. True   *Explanation*: the Europeans would have looked across the Atlantic and the Japanese across the Pacific when the adage that when the United States sneezes the rest of the world catches a cold was true.

84. False   *Explanation*: evidence in support of the hypotheses that when the United States sneezes the rest of the world no longer catches a cold would not show a link between a US recession and a downturn in the rest of the world.

85. False   *Explanation*: in the passage the weather last week is described as balmy, ending in a cold snap. 'Balmy' means mild, so the week was mild but ended cold.

86. False   *Explanation*: it is true that you cannot tell if it snowed this March but you cannot infer from the passage if snow in March is unusual. The passage states that March can bring snow or warm weather.

87. Cannot tell   *Explanation*: the passage does not say if the flowers were early or not and we can't infer whether they were from the passage either.

88. Cannot tell   *Explanation*: that hydroelectric schemes in temperate regions are less polluting may be the consequence of a number of causes and the passage does not provide an explanation.

89. True   *Explanation*: the passage reports that the United Nations wants experts to examine the emissions produced by existing schemes and to recommend ways in which they can be made more environmentally friendly before more are built. It is reasonable to infer therefore that the United Nations does not think hydroelectric power is always a greener power source than alternatives.

90. Cannot tell   *Explanation*: there is not sufficient information provided in the passage to confirm the truth or falsehood of the claim in the statement that methane is the greenhouse gas responsible for the emissions.

91. False   *Explanation*: the passage states that the law will mean that all public bodies will have new responsibilities; by this it is meant governments and organizations providing services paid for from public funds, and a supermarket is not a public body.

92. False   *Explanation*: in respect of public services, while it is true that men and women often have different needs it cannot be inferred from the passage that this is the reason for the different experience men and women have of a service provided under a gender-neutral policy. It may be, for example, that the policy, while seemingly neutral, is not.

93. False   *Explanation*: this is a subordinate idea of the passage; the main one is that men and women should be treated equally.

94. True   *Explanation*: this is a valid summary of the author's intention.

95. False   *Explanation*: an implied definition of 'spam' as unsolicited might be inferred from the passage but this is not a subordinate idea offered in the passage. An example of a subordinate idea from the passage would be the amount of spam doubling to the point where 19 out of 20 e-mails were unsolicited.

96. True   *Explanation*: the term used in the passage was 'seemed incredible', which means hard to believe. The passage states that 19 out of 20 e-mails were unsolicited, so this means only one in 20 were solicited, which is 5 per cent. Sorry to introduce maths, but verbal reasoning routinely involves the valid restatement or summary of numerical data. In business pretty much every e-mail, report or presentation will make reference to numerical data and will be judged better for it. So don't be surprised if some occurs at the periphery of a verbal reasoning test.

97. Cannot tell   *Explanation*: the outcome of the study is not reported in the passage and cannot be inferred from it.

98. False   *Explanation*: from the passage you can infer that the study is authoritative, definitive even, but we cannot infer from the passage if it is the most authoritative in the sense of the best study yet. Other studies may have been as authoritative or carried greater authority in respect of the reputation of the authors or some other feature.

99. True   *Explanation*: the passage states that mobile phones were introduced 20 years ago and fears of a link between their use and cancer have persisted throughout that period. It also states that the extent and duration of the new study means we can have great confidence in the result.

100. False   *Explanation*: the occurrence of more than 15,000 tumours would imply a link between using mobiles and the risk of cancer, but it would not weaken the conclusion of the passage because the passage does not comment on whether or not a link exists.

Chapter 7. Five timed realistic tests with interpretations of your score

Test 1. Synonyms and antonyms

1. B   *Explanation*: the first pair are synonyms as are plebiscite and referendum.
2. C   *Explanation*: lucid and intelligible are synonyms as are static and stationary (stationery is the often confused word meaning pens and paper, etc needed for writing).
3. B   *Explanation*: malicious and commendatory are antonyms as are clamorous and muted.
4. A   *Explanation*: archaic and dated are synonyms as are integral and requisite.
5. B   *Explanation*: veto and interdict are synonyms as are ratify and endorse.
6. A   *Explanation*: momentous and customary are antonyms as are prosperous and distressed.
7. A   *Explanation*: Emulate and echo are synonyms as are apostrophe and punctuation.
8. B   *Explanation*: naïve and sophisticated are antonyms as are sophisticate and provincial.
9. C   *Explanation*: autocratic and enlightened are antonyms as are relinquish and withhold.
10. B   *Explanation*: come by and procure are synonyms as are adolescent and juvenile.
11. A   *Explanation*: fluent and inarticulate are antonyms as are exhilarating and banal.
12. C   *Explanation*: amble and hasten are antonyms as are aligned and neutral.
13. A   *Explanation*: parentheses are punctuation marks that enclose information, ie ( ), a gerund is a noun ending in '-ing' that is verb-like.
14. B   *Explanation*: sanguine and optimistic are synonyms as are gloomy and melancholy.

15. A *Explanation*: limited and incalculable are antonyms as are inimitable and homogeneous.

16. C *Explanation*: simile and paradox are both examples of figures of speech or forms of expression. A simile is used to relate two unlike things, while a paradox is a statement that seems contradictory but in fact has meaning.

17. B *Explanation*: allegra and glum are antonyms as are irascible and cordial.

18. A *Explanation*: allegory and metaphor are synonyms as are chasm and fissure.

19. B *Explanation*: brilliant and inept are antonyms as are remiss and attentive.

20. C *Explanation*: conqueror and vanquisher are synonyms as are caucus and nucleus.

21. B *Explanation*: fruitful and futile are antonyms as are inevitable and ambivalent.

22. C *Explanation*: compliant and recalcitrant are antonyms as are hub and façade.

23. A *Explanation*: condescending and contemptuous are synonyms as are miniscule and diminutive.

24. B *Explanation*: prophecy and forecast are synonyms as are ricochet and bounce.

25. C *Explanation*: relegate and promote are antonyms as are augment and understate.

26. A *Explanation*: idealistic and pragmatic are antonyms as are vertical and width.

27. C *Explanation*: couple and brace are synonyms as are debacle and farce.

28. A *Explanation*: unrelenting and half-hearted are antonyms as are automatic and conscious.

29. A *Explanation*: privation and want are synonyms as are good humoured and amiable.

30. C *Explanation*: dreary and wretched are synonyms as are singular and uncommon.

31. A *Explanation*: rebuke and commend are antonyms as are numerous and few.

32 C *Explanation*: noiselessly and audibly are antonyms as are postscript and prologue.

33. B *Explanation*: lesson and subside are synonyms as are raw and naïve.

34. B *Explanation*: accomplished and incompetent are antonyms as are inconsequential and momentous.

35. C *Explanation*: supplicate and appeal are synonyms as are recess and gap.

36. A *Explanation*: lethargy and vigour are antonyms as are somewhat and greatly.

37. B *Explanation*: exorbitant and inflated are synonyms as are roe and ovum (meaning egg).

38. A *Explanation*: confident and tremulous are antonyms as are provide and refuse.

39. C *Explanation*: animosity and rancour are synonyms as are straighten and settle.

40. B *Explanation*: recommence and suspend are antonyms as are nonchalant and beleaguered.

Test 2. Sentence sequence

1. DACB	2. BDAC	3. BDAC
4. DCBA	5. CBDA	6. BDCA
7. CBAD	8. DCAB	9. CBDA
10. BDCA	11. CADB	12. BADC
13. ADCB	14. BADC	15. CBAD
16. DBCA	17. CDBA	18. BADC
19. CADB	20. DBCA	21. CABD
22. ABCD	23. DABC	24. CBDA
25. BCDA	26. DACB	27. CADB
28. BDAC	29. DBCA	30. CBDA
31. DCBA	32. BADC	33. CADB
34. ACDB	35. ADCB	36. ABDC
37. CBAD	38. DCAB	39. ABCD
40. BADC		

Test 3. Word swap

1. she and who
2. substances and vegetables
3. drink and drinks
4. residues and pesticides (you cannot stop using residues)
5. component and per cent
6. (first) beautiful and intended
7. Poles and immigrants
8. bay and acres
9. elsewhere and will
10. implement and develop
11. (first) in and between
12. when and it
13. pulses and lentils
14. wet and warm
15. and and between
16. only and both
17. discovered and confirmed
18. two and one
19. were and was
20. conventional and hybrid
21. evolutionary and important
22. refinement and combination
23. (first) business and cashflow
24. management and successful
25. death and stroke
26. valuable and record
27. carrying and sent
28. would and said
29. disasters and earthquakes
30. leave and moving
31. achievements and research
32. law and justice
33. held and campaigned
34. nurture and talent

35. were and where
36. (first) many and few
37. figures and citizens
38. their and (second) that
39. seemed and seem
40. inevitable and (third) a

Test 4. English usage

1. D   *Explanation*: we say 'loudly' to mean a noise and 'aloud' when something is spoken rather than read without speaking. B does not make sense.

2. A   *Explanation*: 'because of' is wrong in B but correct in the structure used in D. Answer A is correct because when counting back in time we say 'ago' and not 'before'.

3. D   *Explanation*: an oxymoron occurs when two words have opposite meanings (kindness and suffocating) but when used together they make sense.

4. B   *Explanation*: 'permitted' is more formal but otherwise means the same as 'let' and 'allowed', but in this case the sentence is constructed in the passive form, which is formal, so the correct answer is 'permitted'.

5. B   *Explanation*: the marriage of 20 years continues from the past until the future (next Wednesday) so the future perfect tense 'will have been' is correct.

6. D   *Explanation*: we can say 'pretty well', 'nearly', 'almost', 'very nearly' and 'practically', but not 'very almost', 'pretty well almost' or 'nearly practically'.

7. A   *Explanation*: we only say 'over' and 'below' when something is literally over or under another thing, otherwise we say 'above' or 'below'.

8. B   *Explanation*: we would say 'didn't' if we had something to do but did not do it, and 'mustn't' if something was not allowed. Because the announcement did not occur until after the work was done we can infer that they did work over the

weekend and if we do something that was not necessary we say 'needn't'.

9. D   *Explanation*: 'or else' means 'otherwise', 'all else' means 'all other'. 'Effective' means it works, while 'efficient' means no effort is wasted.

10. B   *Explanation*: expressing irony involves saying the opposite to what is intended or expected. If he was really not hungry, then you would not expect him to order so much food.

11. D   *Explanation*: 'loose' means movable, 'lose' means misplace. We say 'to' something rather than 'till'.

12. C   *Explanation*: always mention the other person or persons first and leave yourself last. Put the completed action first and the second action in the past tense.

13. C   *Explanation*: we say that we play or stand *in* the rain, not *under* it.

14. B   *Explanation*: when making a comparison avoid mixing infinitive and finite forms of verbs.

15. A   *Explanation*: 'a few' means 'some', while 'few' means 'not many'; likewise 'a little' and 'little' mean 'some' and 'few' but are correctly used when referring to uncountable nouns.

16. D   *Explanation*: to refuse is to not take something offered, to deny is to answer in the negative. A proposition should properly follow the direct object.

17. A   *Explanation*: when the main clause is in the past tense we use 'would'.

18. A   *Explanation*: we use the present simple tense when describing something we do. D is incorrect because it does not make sense.

19. C   *Explanation*: 'shadow' refers to shade of a particular shape, while we use 'middle' rather than 'centre' if we are not suggesting accuracy.

20. D   *Explanation*: the information about dog breeds is irrelevant to the question, which is investigating the misuse of two negatives. Two negatives should be avoided as they change the sense to affirmative, so A and B are grammatically incorrect. C does not make sense.

21. B   *Explanation*: when an event is happening at the time of speaking we use the present continuous: enjoying, doing, etc.

22. B   *Explanation*: 'price' is that paid by the customer, while 'cost' is the amount paid at wholesale.

23. D   *Explanation*: when we refer to a period that continues to the present we use the present perfect: 'travelled', 'been', 'visited'.

24. A   *Explanation*: you can die *of* hunger but not *from* hunger. You can die *of* or *from* the wounds received *in* but not *by* battle.

25. C   *Explanation*: 'do' and 'does 'are the present simple tense, which we use to talk in general about things that happen all the time. We use 'do' when we refer to ourselves, you and they, and 'does' for the third person and for inanimate objects: we, he, she or it.

26. D   *Explanation*: we can correctly say either 'tell me' or 'say', but we must identify the subject in both cases as they are different.

27. B   *Explanation*: the deal is still not closed, so we say 'have been' rather than 'has worked'.

28. A   *Explanation*: we use 'keep' or 'kept' when referring to something permanent, and 'made of' when the material is identifiable. We would prefer 'made from' when, for example, the process of manufacture made it impossible to identify the material.

29. B   *Explanation*: both 'scissors' and 'pair of scissors' are correct, but we don't use the singular 'scissor' (we often use 'pair' when referring to things made from two parts). The plural of 'child' is the irregular 'children'.

30. A   *Explanation*: 'do you like' means 'do you enjoy some-thing'; 'do you want' enquires into your wishes, 'would want' or 'would like' are more polite but it does not make sense as phrased in the other suggested answers.

31. D   *Explanation*: 'at present' means 'now', while 'presently' means 'soon'. It is incorrect to say *before* two weeks; we would say two weeks *ago*.

32. C   *Explanation*: use 'many' for plural nouns and 'much' for uncountable nouns.

33. B   *Explanation*: we use 'elder' when referring to people, especially relatives, but not if followed by the word 'than'.

34. D   *Explanation*: we could say 'too bitter' or 'very bitter' but not 'much bitter' ('very' would be used for emphasis). We use 'each' when referring to the individual and 'every' to a group.

35. A   *Explanation*: the original came first so it is different *to* not *from* the sequel. 'Than' is a conjunction, so is incorrect when making a comparison. The film would be guilty *of* not *for*.

36. C   *Explanation*: we use the present continuous – rising, doing, working, etc – when we refer to something happening at the time of speaking or writing.

37. C   *Explanation*: we correctly say either 'visits to' or 'visiting'. 'Kind' is singular, so this must agree with 'it' rather than 'these'.

38. A   *Explanation*: 'all' meaning 'everybody' takes a plural verb, while 'all' meaning 'everything' takes a singular verb.

39. B   *Explanation*: we would correctly say 'afterwards' and use the adjective 'open', not the past participle 'opened'.

40. D   *Explanation*: we do not use the present continuous tense in the case of 'thinking' (it is not an action like doing); instead we use the present continuous 'think'.

Test 5. Reading comprehension and critical reasoning

1. False *Explanation*: it cannot be inferred that trace levels of Acrylamide are toxic. The levels at which the animal studies found it to be a carcinogen are not stated nor can they be inferred. The passage states that an urgent search began to establish the risk and this suggests that the extent to which trace levels might prove toxic are unknown.

2. Cannot tell *Explanation*: we are told that it was 2002 when news of the presence of Acrylamide in many foodstuffs emerged and the passage states that an urgent search had begun, but the date that the passage was written is not know nor are we given an indication of the timescale in which answers might be found. For these reasons it cannot be known if the author would disagree (or agree) with the view that answers to the questions raised about the safety of Acrylamide should by now be close to being found.

3. False *Explanation*: the issue of how difficult it might prove to remove the substance from the human food chain has no bearing on the likelihood that the ingestion of Acrylamide poses a health risk.

4. Cannot tell *Explanation*: it is not stated in the passage whether or not Britain will realize its Kyoto target, nor can this information be inferred from the passage.

5. False *Explanation*: the passage does not state this, but that emissions would be lower if more radical policies had been adopted can be inferred from the passage. But the question does not ask what can be *inferred* from the passage, only what is *stated* in the passage.

6. True *Explanation*: the passage starts with the announcement of 1997 and the progress made towards the target until 2002; it then considers the setback after 2002 and the admission of failure to realize the target in 2005. Thus it is true to say that the passage follows events chronologically.

7. True   *Explanation*: it is stated in the passage that political parties should vote to increase taxpayers' support; it can be inferred from this that there is already a state subsidy paid.

8. False   *Explanation*: the second sentence of the passage states the details of the compromise, not the stand-off.

9. True   *Explanation*: reference is made in the details of the compromise to the cap or ceiling to donations, but it is not suggested or inferred that agreement has been reached over this point. Equally there is nothing in the passage that suggests the parties may not remain divided over the issue of spending limits on both local and national elections.

10. True   *Explanation*: the passage states that Yulia Tymoshenko split from the 'Our Ukraine Party' to run her own election campaign.

11. True   *Explanation*: while it is clear from the passage that 'The Party of Regions' received the highest percentage of votes, the passage states that 'the result means that the next government of the Ukraine is likely to be a coalition' and from this we can infer that the election failed to produce an outright winner.

12. Cannot tell   *Explanation*: the passage states that Tymoshenko was sacked from a ministerial post and split from the 'Our Ukraine Party' and it also states that the President and leader of the 'Our Ukraine Party' is Mr Yushchenko, but it cannot be inferred from this that is was necessarily Mr Yushchenko who sacked Ms Tymoshenko.

13. True   *Explanation*: an ambidextrous person is able to use right and left hands equally well. The passage describes the ambidextrous dogs as showing no preference for left or right.

14. False   *Explanation*: the case made in the passage would be greatly *weakened* if this characteristic was manifest before the dogs began training as there would be no need for a new test.

15. True   *Explanation*: such a test would be of commercial interest because it could reduce the number of dogs that start training but are later found to develop this undesirable characteristic.

16. False   *Explanation*: the main theme (point) of the passage is to describe how the planned closure of 2,500 rural post offices will greatly worsen rural isolation.

17. True   *Explanation*: the passage opens with a definition of rural isolation as a lack of access to essential economic and social components and then goes on to illustrate that isolation with examples from public transport and access to shops and government services.

18. Cannot tell   *Explanation*: the author is likely to agree that there is a risk of this occurring, but we cannot tell if the author would agree that a community shop would close if the post office based in it is closed.

19. False   *Explanation*: the passage states that animals in the tropics exhibit fewer seasonal variations in behaviour and therefore it is not true to say that *all* animals dramatically adapt their behaviour to suit the seasons.

20. False   *Explanation*: the passage does not provide an explanation as to why tropical animals' behaviour is less sensitive to the season.

21. True   *Explanation*: the author refers to shift-workers and long-distance flyers generally as well as most workers and children in northern latitudes.

22. Cannot tell   *Explanation*: the passage does not provide any detail of the environmentalists' campaign against the 4x4 and so we are unable to tell if the research findings would undermine that campaign.

23. False   *Explanation*: the passage states that people were put off by the high running costs of these vehicles, suggesting that the passage is based on the assumption that 4x4s are fuel inefficient, but the passage is not based on any assumption regarding the relative inefficiency of these cases compared with older types of car.

24. True   *Explanation*: it is stated in the passage that existing owners face significant losses should they decide to sell, and from this we can deduce that second-hand values have dropped significantly.

25. False   *Explanation*: the passage does not state that it was a surprise that the number of new cases should fall but that the rate and speed of the fall was a surprise.

26. True   *Explanation*: it would be wrong because the rise in cases over two decades is attributed to two factors – the aging population and screening – and we do not know which effect was responsible for the increase of new cases at which time.

27. True   *Explanation*: 'contingent' means true by the way things are rather than logically true, and the passage describes a factual association between the fall in cases and the decrease in the number of women taking the therapy.

28. True   *Explanation*: this is a valid restatement of the opening sentences. The forbear who believed the moon was really the size it appears in the sky would not want to create the impression of depth for his picture to be representational.

29. False   *Explanation*: while we can infer that the ancient Egyptians did not share our need to create the illusion of depth in their paintings, this does not allow us to conclude that they never created the illusion in their perspective in the art.

30. True   *Explanation*: the example given describes two methods; 'if parallel lines are shown to converge' and objects 'at a distance are depicted as smaller'.

31. False   *Explanation*: the author *would* agree with this statement as it is consistent with the statement made in the passage that the citizens of these countries hold 90 per cent of the world's wealth.

32. False   *Explanation*: the passage does not make the assumption that the world's poor live in certain countries as it acknowledges that within the wealth zones of the United States and Europe there is inequality between rich and poor.

33. Cannot tell *Explanation*: the passage does not comment on the risk of tension created by the inequity and whether or not such tension exists cannot be inferred either.
34. Cannot tell *Explanation*: the geographic location of the porcelain is not identified in the passage.
35. False *Explanation*: the passage does not provide details on the relative popularity of the white and later painted porcelain.
36. False *Explanation*: the passage describes the colour of the porcelain that utilized the newly discovered Persian cobalt as blue and white, not green.
37. False *Explanation*: it is clear from the passage that the term 'serious crime' *includes* the offences of murder and attempted murder, but it is not possible to infer that the term can be defined to mean murder and attempted murder.
38. False *Explanation*: the passage argues that serious crime is committed by criminals on probation because they are released early, not because they are inadequately supervised.
39. Cannot tell *Explanation*: murder can happen in prison as well as when a person is under the supervision of the probation service, so we cannot know if 100 murders would have been avoided or not.
40. False *Explanation*: 100 years ago washing machines and running hot water would not have featured in a list of indicators of poverty.
41. True *Explanation*: if the definition of poverty is set according to a middle (median) income value, then it is possible that the number of people who are classed as poor will increase if they do not keep up with the rate at which society's wealth increases.
42. True *Explanation*: according to the passage this would be an acceptable definition of absolute poverty and people would not be poor in absolute terms if they are fed, clothed and housed.